LAWN CARE CLIENT LOG

BUSINESS/COMPANY NAME

ADDRESS

CONTACT

LOG BOOK INFORMATION

START DATE	END DATE

INFORMATIONS

DATE: .... TIME: .... S M T W TH F S

CLIENT NAME	
PHONE NO	
EMAIL	
ADDRESS/ CITY-STATE-ZIP	

JOB FREQUENCY	WEEKLY /BI-WEEKLY	MONTHLY / BI-MONTHLY
PAYMENT PERIODS	○ WEEKLY ○ MONTHLY	○ 6-MO ○ YEARLY
FEE AMOUNT		

SERVICES

○ MOWING	○ FERTILIZING	○ TREE TRIMMING PRUNING
○ WEED EATING	○ BLOWING	○ POWER WASHING
○ EDGING	○ MULCHING	○ PEST CONTROL
○ HEDGE TRIMMING	○ WEEDING	○ GUTTER CLEANING
○ WATERING	○ LEAF/STRAW RAKING	○ AERATION

INSTRUCTIONS

TOOLS

INFORMATIONS

DATE: .... TIME: .... S M T W TH F S

CLIENT NAME	
PHONE NO	
EMAIL	
ADDRESS/ CITY-STATE-ZIP	

JOB FREQUENCY	WEEKLY /BI-WEEKLY	MONTHLY / BI-MONTHLY
PAYMENT PERIODS	○ WEEKLY ○ MONTHLY	○ 6-MO ○ YEARLY
FEE AMOUNT		

SERVICES

○ MOWING	○ FERTILIZING	○ TREE TRIMMING PRUNING
○ WEED EATING	○ BLOWING	○ POWER WASHING
○ EDGING	○ MULCHING	○ PEST CONTROL
○ HEDGE TRIMMING	○ WEEDING	○ GUTTER CLEANING
○ WATERING	○ LEAF/STRAW RAKING	○ AERATION

INSTRUCTIONS

TOOLS

INFORMATIONS

DATE: .... TIME: .... S M T W TH F S

CLIENT NAME	
PHONE NO	
EMAIL	
ADDRESS/ CITY-STATE-ZIP	

JOB FREQUENCY	WEEKLY /BI-WEEKLY	MONTHLY / BI-MONTHLY
PAYMENT PERIODS	○ WEEKLY　　○ MONTHLY	○ 6-MO　　○ YEARLY
FEE AMOUNT		

SERVICES

○ MOWING	○ FERTILIZING	○ TREE TRIMMING PRUNING
○ WEED EATING	○ BLOWING	○ POWER WASHING
○ EDGING	○ MULCHING	○ PEST CONTROL
○ HEDGE TRIMMING	○ WEEDING	○ GUTTER CLEANING
○ WATERING	○ LEAF/STRAW RAKING	○ AERATION

INSTRUCTIONS

TOOLS

INFORMATIONS

DATE: .... TIME: .... S M T W TH F S

CLIENT NAME	
PHONE NO	
EMAIL	
ADDRESS/ CITY-STATE-ZIP	

JOB FREQUENCY	WEEKLY /BI-WEEKLY	MONTHLY / BI-MONTHLY
PAYMENT PERIODS	○ WEEKLY ○ MONTHLY	○ 6-MO ○ YEARLY
FEE AMOUNT		

SERVICES

○ MOWING	○ FERTILIZING	○ TREE TRIMMING PRUNING
○ WEED EATING	○ BLOWING	○ POWER WASHING
○ EDGING	○ MULCHING	○ PEST CONTROL
○ HEDGE TRIMMING	○ WEEDING	○ GUTTER CLEANING
○ WATERING	○ LEAF/STRAW RAKING	○ AERATION

INSTRUCTIONS

TOOLS

INFORMATIONS

DATE: .... TIME: .... S M T W TH F S

CLIENT NAME	
PHONE NO	
EMAIL	
ADDRESS/ CITY-STATE-ZIP	

JOB FREQUENCY	WEEKLY /BI-WEEKLY	MONTHLY / BI-MONTHLY
PAYMENT PERIODS	○ WEEKLY ○ MONTHLY	○ 6-MO ○ YEARLY
FEE AMOUNT		

SERVICES

○ MOWING	○ FERTILIZING	○ TREE TRIMMING PRUNING
○ WEED EATING	○ BLOWING	○ POWER WASHING
○ EDGING	○ MULCHING	○ PEST CONTROL
○ HEDGE TRIMMING	○ WEEDING	○ GUTTER CLEANING
○ WATERING	○ LEAF/STRAW RAKING	○ AERATION

INSTRUCTIONS

TOOLS

INFORMATIONS

DATE: .... TIME: .... S M T W TH F S

CLIENT NAME	
PHONE NO	
EMAIL	
ADDRESS/ CITY-STATE-ZIP	

JOB FREQUENCY	WEEKLY /BI-WEEKLY	MONTHLY / BI-MONTHLY
PAYMENT PERIODS	○ WEEKLY ○ MONTHLY	○ 6-MO ○ YEARLY
FEE AMOUNT		

SERVICES

○ MOWING
○ WEED EATING
○ EDGING
○ HEDGE TRIMMING
○ WATERING

○ FERTILIZING
○ BLOWING
○ MULCHING
○ WEEDING
○ LEAF/STRAW RAKING

○ TREE TRIMMING PRUNING
○ POWER WASHING
○ PEST CONTROL
○ GUTTER CLEANING
○ AERATION

INSTRUCTIONS

TOOLS

INFORMATIONS

DATE: .... TIME: .... S M T W TH F S

CLIENT NAME	
PHONE NO	
EMAIL	
ADDRESS/ CITY-STATE-ZIP	

JOB FREQUENCY	WEEKLY /BI-WEEKLY	MONTHLY / BI-MONTHLY
PAYMENT PERIODS	○ WEEKLY ○ MONTHLY	○ 6-MO ○ YEARLY
FEE AMOUNT		

SERVICES

○ MOWING	○ FERTILIZING	○ TREE TRIMMING PRUNING
○ WEED EATING	○ BLOWING	○ POWER WASHING
○ EDGING	○ MULCHING	○ PEST CONTROL
○ HEDGE TRIMMING	○ WEEDING	○ GUTTER CLEANING
○ WATERING	○ LEAF/STRAW RAKING	○ AERATION

INSTRUCTIONS

TOOLS

INFORMATIONS

DATE: .... TIME: .... S M T W TH F S

CLIENT NAME	
PHONE NO	
EMAIL	
ADDRESS/ CITY-STATE-ZIP	

JOB FREQUENCY	WEEKLY /BI-WEEKLY	MONTHLY / BI-MONTHLY
PAYMENT PERIODS	◯ WEEKLY ◯ MONTHLY	◯ 6-MO ◯ YEARLY
FEE AMOUNT		

SERVICES

◯ MOWING	◯ FERTILIZING	◯ TREE TRIMMING PRUNING
◯ WEED EATING	◯ BLOWING	◯ POWER WASHING
◯ EDGING	◯ MULCHING	◯ PEST CONTROL
◯ HEDGE TRIMMING	◯ WEEDING	◯ GUTTER CLEANING
◯ WATERING	◯ LEAF/STRAW RAKING	◯ AERATION

INSTRUCTIONS

TOOLS

INFORMATIONS

DATE: .... TIME: .... S M T W TH F S

CLIENT NAME	
PHONE NO	
EMAIL	
ADDRESS/ CITY-STATE-ZIP	

JOB FREQUENCY	WEEKLY /BI-WEEKLY	MONTHLY / BI-MONTHLY
PAYMENT PERIODS	○ WEEKLY ○ MONTHLY	○ 6-MO ○ YEARLY
FEE AMOUNT		

SERVICES

○ MOWING	○ FERTILIZING	○ TREE TRIMMING PRUNING
○ WEED EATING	○ BLOWING	○ POWER WASHING
○ EDGING	○ MULCHING	○ PEST CONTROL
○ HEDGE TRIMMING	○ WEEDING	○ GUTTER CLEANING
○ WATERING	○ LEAF/STRAW RAKING	○ AERATION

INSTRUCTIONS

TOOLS

INFORMATIONS

DATE: .... TIME: .... S M T W TH F S

CLIENT NAME	
PHONE NO	
EMAIL	
ADDRESS/ CITY-STATE-ZIP	

JOB FREQUENCY	WEEKLY /BI-WEEKLY	MONTHLY / BI-MONTHLY
PAYMENT PERIODS	○ WEEKLY ○ MONTHLY	○ 6-MO ○ YEARLY
FEE AMOUNT		

SERVICES

○ MOWING	○ FERTILIZING	○ TREE TRIMMING PRUNING
○ WEED EATING	○ BLOWING	○ POWER WASHING
○ EDGING	○ MULCHING	○ PEST CONTROL
○ HEDGE TRIMMING	○ WEEDING	○ GUTTER CLEANING
○ WATERING	○ LEAF/STRAW RAKING	○ AERATION

INSTRUCTIONS

TOOLS

INFORMATIONS

DATE: .... TIME: .... S M T W TH F S

CLIENT NAME	
PHONE NO	
EMAIL	
ADDRESS/ CITY-STATE-ZIP	

JOB FREQUENCY	WEEKLY /BI-WEEKLY	MONTHLY / BI-MONTHLY
PAYMENT PERIODS	◯ WEEKLY ◯ MONTHLY	◯ 6-MO ◯ YEARLY
FEE AMOUNT		

SERVICES

◯ MOWING	◯ FERTILIZING	◯ TREE TRIMMING PRUNING
◯ WEED EATING	◯ BLOWING	◯ POWER WASHING
◯ EDGING	◯ MULCHING	◯ PEST CONTROL
◯ HEDGE TRIMMING	◯ WEEDING	◯ GUTTER CLEANING
◯ WATERING	◯ LEAF/STRAW RAKING	◯ AERATION

INSTRUCTIONS

TOOLS

INFORMATIONS

DATE: .... TIME: .... S M T W TH F S

CLIENT NAME	
PHONE NO	
EMAIL	
ADDRESS/ CITY-STATE-ZIP	

JOB FREQUENCY	WEEKLY /BI-WEEKLY	MONTHLY / BI-MONTHLY
PAYMENT PERIODS	◯ WEEKLY ◯ MONTHLY	◯ 6-MO ◯ YEARLY
FEE AMOUNT		

SERVICES

◯ MOWING	◯ FERTILIZING	◯ TREE TRIMMING PRUNING
◯ WEED EATING	◯ BLOWING	◯ POWER WASHING
◯ EDGING	◯ MULCHING	◯ PEST CONTROL
◯ HEDGE TRIMMING	◯ WEEDING	◯ GUTTER CLEANING
◯ WATERING	◯ LEAF/STRAW RAKING	◯ AERATION

INSTRUCTIONS

TOOLS

INFORMATIONS

DATE: .... TIME: .... S M T W TH F S

CLIENT NAME	
PHONE NO	
EMAIL	
ADDRESS/ CITY-STATE-ZIP	

JOB FREQUENCY	WEEKLY /BI-WEEKLY	MONTHLY / BI-MONTHLY
PAYMENT PERIODS	○ WEEKLY ○ MONTHLY	○ 6-MO ○ YEARLY
FEE AMOUNT		

SERVICES

○ MOWING	○ FERTILIZING	○ TREE TRIMMING PRUNING
○ WEED EATING	○ BLOWING	○ POWER WASHING
○ EDGING	○ MULCHING	○ PEST CONTROL
○ HEDGE TRIMMING	○ WEEDING	○ GUTTER CLEANING
○ WATERING	○ LEAF/STRAW RAKING	○ AERATION

INSTRUCTIONS

TOOLS

INFORMATIONS

DATE: .... TIME: ....   S   M   T   W   TH   F   S

CLIENT NAME	
PHONE NO	
EMAIL	
ADDRESS/ CITY-STATE-ZIP	

JOB FREQUENCY	WEEKLY /BI-WEEKLY	MONTHLY / BI-MONTHLY
PAYMENT PERIODS	○ WEEKLY ○ MONTHLY	○ 6-MO ○ YEARLY
FEE AMOUNT		

SERVICES

○ MOWING	○ FERTILIZING	○ TREE TRIMMING PRUNING
○ WEED EATING	○ BLOWING	○ POWER WASHING
○ EDGING	○ MULCHING	○ PEST CONTROL
○ HEDGE TRIMMING	○ WEEDING	○ GUTTER CLEANING
○ WATERING	○ LEAF/STRAW RAKING	○ AERATION

INSTRUCTIONS

TOOLS

INFORMATIONS

DATE: .... TIME: .... S M T W TH F S

CLIENT NAME	
PHONE NO	
EMAIL	
ADDRESS/ CITY-STATE-ZIP	

JOB FREQUENCY	WEEKLY /BI-WEEKLY	MONTHLY / BI-MONTHLY
PAYMENT PERIODS	○ WEEKLY ○ MONTHLY	○ 6-MO ○ YEARLY
FEE AMOUNT		

SERVICES

○ MOWING	○ FERTILIZING	○ TREE TRIMMING PRUNING
○ WEED EATING	○ BLOWING	○ POWER WASHING
○ EDGING	○ MULCHING	○ PEST CONTROL
○ HEDGE TRIMMING	○ WEEDING	○ GUTTER CLEANING
○ WATERING	○ LEAF/STRAW RAKING	○ AERATION

INSTRUCTIONS

TOOLS

INFORMATIONS

DATE: .... **TIME:** .... S M T W TH F S

CLIENT NAME	
PHONE NO	
EMAIL	
ADDRESS/ CITY-STATE-ZIP	

JOB FREQUENCY	WEEKLY /BI-WEEKLY	MONTHLY / BI-MONTHLY
PAYMENT PERIODS	○ WEEKLY ○ MONTHLY	○ 6-MO ○ YEARLY
FEE AMOUNT		

SERVICES

○ MOWING
○ WEED EATING
○ EDGING
○ HEDGE TRIMMING
○ WATERING

○ FERTILIZING
○ BLOWING
○ MULCHING
○ WEEDING
○ LEAF/STRAW RAKING

○ TREE TRIMMING PRUNING
○ POWER WASHING
○ PEST CONTROL
○ GUTTER CLEANING
○ AERATION

INSTRUCTIONS

TOOLS

INFORMATIONS

DATE: .... TIME: .... S M T W TH F S

CLIENT NAME	
PHONE NO	
EMAIL	
ADDRESS/ CITY-STATE-ZIP	

JOB FREQUENCY	WEEKLY /BI-WEEKLY	MONTHLY / BI-MONTHLY
PAYMENT PERIODS	○ WEEKLY ○ MONTHLY	○ 6-MO ○ YEARLY
FEE AMOUNT		

SERVICES

○ MOWING	○ FERTILIZING	○ TREE TRIMMING PRUNING
○ WEED EATING	○ BLOWING	○ POWER WASHING
○ EDGING	○ MULCHING	○ PEST CONTROL
○ HEDGE TRIMMING	○ WEEDING	○ GUTTER CLEANING
○ WATERING	○ LEAF/STRAW RAKING	○ AERATION

INSTRUCTIONS

TOOLS

INFORMATIONS

DATE: .... TIME: .... S M T W TH F S

CLIENT NAME	
PHONE NO	
EMAIL	
ADDRESS/ CITY-STATE-ZIP	

JOB FREQUENCY	WEEKLY /BI-WEEKLY	MONTHLY / BI-MONTHLY
PAYMENT PERIODS	○ WEEKLY ○ MONTHLY	○ 6-MO ○ YEARLY
FEE AMOUNT		

SERVICES

○ MOWING	○ FERTILIZING	○ TREE TRIMMING PRUNING
○ WEED EATING	○ BLOWING	○ POWER WASHING
○ EDGING	○ MULCHING	○ PEST CONTROL
○ HEDGE TRIMMING	○ WEEDING	○ GUTTER CLEANING
○ WATERING	○ LEAF/STRAW RAKING	○ AERATION

INSTRUCTIONS

TOOLS

DATE: .... TIME: .... S M T W TH F S

CLIENT NAME	
PHONE NO	
EMAIL	
ADDRESS/ CITY-STATE-ZIP	

JOB FREQUENCY	WEEKLY /BI-WEEKLY	MONTHLY / BI-MONTHLY
PAYMENT PERIODS	○ WEEKLY ○ MONTHLY	○ 6-MO ○ YEARLY
FEE AMOUNT		

SERVICES

○ MOWING	○ FERTILIZING	○ TREE TRIMMING PRUNING
○ WEED EATING	○ BLOWING	○ POWER WASHING
○ EDGING	○ MULCHING	○ PEST CONTROL
○ HEDGE TRIMMING	○ WEEDING	○ GUTTER CLEANING
○ WATERING	○ LEAF/STRAW RAKING	○ AERATION

INSTRUCTIONS

TOOLS

INFORMATIONS

DATE: .... TIME: .... S M T W TH F S

CLIENT NAME	
PHONE NO	
EMAIL	
ADDRESS/ CITY-STATE-ZIP	

JOB FREQUENCY	WEEKLY /BI-WEEKLY	MONTHLY / BI-MONTHLY
PAYMENT PERIODS	◯ WEEKLY ◯ MONTHLY	◯ 6-MO ◯ YEARLY
FEE AMOUNT		

SERVICES

◯ MOWING	◯ FERTILIZING	◯ TREE TRIMMING PRUNING
◯ WEED EATING	◯ BLOWING	◯ POWER WASHING
◯ EDGING	◯ MULCHING	◯ PEST CONTROL
◯ HEDGE TRIMMING	◯ WEEDING	◯ GUTTER CLEANING
◯ WATERING	◯ LEAF/STRAW RAKING	◯ AERATION

INSTRUCTIONS

TOOLS

INFORMATIONS

DATE: .... TIME: .... **S M T W TH F S**

CLIENT NAME	
PHONE NO	
EMAIL	
ADDRESS/ CITY-STATE-ZIP	

JOB FREQUENCY	WEEKLY /BI-WEEKLY	MONTHLY / BI-MONTHLY
PAYMENT PERIODS	○ WEEKLY ○ MONTHLY	○ 6-MO ○ YEARLY
FEE AMOUNT		

SERVICES

○ MOWING	○ FERTILIZING	○ TREE TRIMMING PRUNING
○ WEED EATING	○ BLOWING	○ POWER WASHING
○ EDGING	○ MULCHING	○ PEST CONTROL
○ HEDGE TRIMMING	○ WEEDING	○ GUTTER CLEANING
○ WATERING	○ LEAF/STRAW RAKING	○ AERATION

INSTRUCTIONS

TOOLS

INFORMATIONS

DATE: .... TIME: .... S M T W TH F S

CLIENT NAME	
PHONE NO	
EMAIL	
ADDRESS/ CITY-STATE-ZIP	

JOB FREQUENCY	WEEKLY /BI-WEEKLY	MONTHLY / BI-MONTHLY
PAYMENT PERIODS	○ WEEKLY ○ MONTHLY	○ 6-MO ○ YEARLY
FEE AMOUNT		

SERVICES

○ MOWING
○ WEED EATING
○ EDGING
○ HEDGE TRIMMING
○ WATERING

○ FERTILIZING
○ BLOWING
○ MULCHING
○ WEEDING
○ LEAF/STRAW RAKING

○ TREE TRIMMING PRUNING
○ POWER WASHING
○ PEST CONTROL
○ GUTTER CLEANING
○ AERATION

INSTRUCTIONS

TOOLS

INFORMATIONS

DATE: .... TIME: .... S M T W TH F S

CLIENT NAME	
PHONE NO	
EMAIL	
ADDRESS/ CITY-STATE-ZIP	

JOB FREQUENCY	WEEKLY /BI-WEEKLY	MONTHLY / BI-MONTHLY
PAYMENT PERIODS	○ WEEKLY ○ MONTHLY	○ 6-MO ○ YEARLY
FEE AMOUNT		

SERVICES

○ MOWING	○ FERTILIZING	○ TREE TRIMMING PRUNING
○ WEED EATING	○ BLOWING	○ POWER WASHING
○ EDGING	○ MULCHING	○ PEST CONTROL
○ HEDGE TRIMMING	○ WEEDING	○ GUTTER CLEANING
○ WATERING	○ LEAF/STRAW RAKING	○ AERATION

INSTRUCTIONS

TOOLS

INFORMATIONS

DATE: .... TIME: .... S M T W TH F S

CLIENT NAME	
PHONE NO	
EMAIL	
ADDRESS/ CITY-STATE-ZIP	

JOB FREQUENCY	WEEKLY /BI-WEEKLY	MONTHLY / BI-MONTHLY
PAYMENT PERIODS	◯ WEEKLY ◯ MONTHLY	◯ 6-MO ◯ YEARLY
FEE AMOUNT		

SERVICES

◯ MOWING	◯ FERTILIZING	◯ TREE TRIMMING PRUNING
◯ WEED EATING	◯ BLOWING	◯ POWER WASHING
◯ EDGING	◯ MULCHING	◯ PEST CONTROL
◯ HEDGE TRIMMING	◯ WEEDING	◯ GUTTER CLEANING
◯ WATERING	◯ LEAF/STRAW RAKING	◯ AERATION

INSTRUCTIONS

TOOLS

INFORMATIONS

DATE: .... TIME: .... S M T W TH F S

CLIENT NAME	
PHONE NO	
EMAIL	
ADDRESS/ CITY-STATE-ZIP	

JOB FREQUENCY	WEEKLY /BI-WEEKLY	MONTHLY / BI-MONTHLY
PAYMENT PERIODS	○ WEEKLY ○ MONTHLY	○ 6-MO ○ YEARLY
FEE AMOUNT		

SERVICES

○ MOWING	○ FERTILIZING	○ TREE TRIMMING PRUNING
○ WEED EATING	○ BLOWING	○ POWER WASHING
○ EDGING	○ MULCHING	○ PEST CONTROL
○ HEDGE TRIMMING	○ WEEDING	○ GUTTER CLEANING
○ WATERING	○ LEAF/STRAW RAKING	○ AERATION

INSTRUCTIONS

TOOLS

INFORMATIONS

DATE: .... TIME: .... S M T W TH F S

CLIENT NAME	
PHONE NO	
EMAIL	
ADDRESS/ CITY-STATE-ZIP	

JOB FREQUENCY	WEEKLY /BI-WEEKLY	MONTHLY / BI-MONTHLY
PAYMENT PERIODS	○ WEEKLY ○ MONTHLY	○ 6-MO ○ YEARLY
FEE AMOUNT		

SERVICES

○ MOWING	○ FERTILIZING	○ TREE TRIMMING PRUNING
○ WEED EATING	○ BLOWING	○ POWER WASHING
○ EDGING	○ MULCHING	○ PEST CONTROL
○ HEDGE TRIMMING	○ WEEDING	○ GUTTER CLEANING
○ WATERING	○ LEAF/STRAW RAKING	○ AERATION

INSTRUCTIONS

TOOLS

INFORMATIONS

DATE: .... TIME: .... S M T W TH F S

CLIENT NAME	
PHONE NO	
EMAIL	
ADDRESS/ CITY-STATE-ZIP	

JOB FREQUENCY	WEEKLY /BI-WEEKLY	MONTHLY / BI-MONTHLY
PAYMENT PERIODS	○ WEEKLY ○ MONTHLY	○ 6-MO ○ YEARLY
FEE AMOUNT		

SERVICES

○ MOWING	○ FERTILIZING	○ TREE TRIMMING PRUNING
○ WEED EATING	○ BLOWING	○ POWER WASHING
○ EDGING	○ MULCHING	○ PEST CONTROL
○ HEDGE TRIMMING	○ WEEDING	○ GUTTER CLEANING
○ WATERING	○ LEAF/STRAW RAKING	○ AERATION

INSTRUCTIONS

TOOLS

INFORMATIONS

DATE: .... TIME: .... S M T W TH F S

CLIENT NAME	
PHONE NO	
EMAIL	
ADDRESS/ CITY-STATE-ZIP	

JOB FREQUENCY	WEEKLY /BI-WEEKLY	MONTHLY / BI-MONTHLY
PAYMENT PERIODS	○ WEEKLY ○ MONTHLY	○ 6-MO ○ YEARLY
FEE AMOUNT		

SERVICES

○ MOWING	○ FERTILIZING	○ TREE TRIMMING PRUNING
○ WEED EATING	○ BLOWING	○ POWER WASHING
○ EDGING	○ MULCHING	○ PEST CONTROL
○ HEDGE TRIMMING	○ WEEDING	○ GUTTER CLEANING
○ WATERING	○ LEAF/STRAW RAKING	○ AERATION

INSTRUCTIONS

TOOLS

INFORMATIONS

DATE: .... **TIME:** .... S M T W TH F S

CLIENT NAME	
PHONE NO	
EMAIL	
ADDRESS/ CITY-STATE-ZIP	

JOB FREQUENCY	WEEKLY /BI-WEEKLY	MONTHLY / BI-MONTHLY
PAYMENT PERIODS	○ WEEKLY ○ MONTHLY	○ 6-MO ○ YEARLY
FEE AMOUNT		

SERVICES

○ MOWING	○ FERTILIZING	○ TREE TRIMMING PRUNING
○ WEED EATING	○ BLOWING	○ POWER WASHING
○ EDGING	○ MULCHING	○ PEST CONTROL
○ HEDGE TRIMMING	○ WEEDING	○ GUTTER CLEANING
○ WATERING	○ LEAF/STRAW RAKING	○ AERATION

INSTRUCTIONS

TOOLS

INFORMATIONS

DATE: .... TIME: .... S M T W TH F S

CLIENT NAME	
PHONE NO	
EMAIL	
ADDRESS/ CITY-STATE-ZIP	

JOB FREQUENCY	WEEKLY /BI-WEEKLY	MONTHLY / BI-MONTHLY
PAYMENT PERIODS	○ WEEKLY ○ MONTHLY	○ 6-MO ○ YEARLY
FEE AMOUNT		

SERVICES

○ MOWING	○ FERTILIZING	○ TREE TRIMMING PRUNING
○ WEED EATING	○ BLOWING	○ POWER WASHING
○ EDGING	○ MULCHING	○ PEST CONTROL
○ HEDGE TRIMMING	○ WEEDING	○ GUTTER CLEANING
○ WATERING	○ LEAF/STRAW RAKING	○ AERATION

INSTRUCTIONS

TOOLS

INFORMATIONS

DATE: .... TIME: .... S M T W TH F S

CLIENT NAME	
PHONE NO	
EMAIL	
ADDRESS/ CITY-STATE-ZIP	

JOB FREQUENCY	WEEKLY /BI-WEEKLY	MONTHLY / BI-MONTHLY
PAYMENT PERIODS	○ WEEKLY ○ MONTHLY	○ 6-MO ○ YEARLY
FEE AMOUNT		

SERVICES

○ MOWING	○ FERTILIZING	○ TREE TRIMMING PRUNING
○ WEED EATING	○ BLOWING	○ POWER WASHING
○ EDGING	○ MULCHING	○ PEST CONTROL
○ HEDGE TRIMMING	○ WEEDING	○ GUTTER CLEANING
○ WATERING	○ LEAF/STRAW RAKING	○ AERATION

INSTRUCTIONS

TOOLS

INFORMATIONS

DATE: .... TIME: ....   S   M   T   W   TH   F   S

CLIENT NAME	
PHONE NO	
EMAIL	
ADDRESS/ CITY-STATE-ZIP	

JOB FREQUENCY	WEEKLY /BI-WEEKLY	MONTHLY / BI-MONTHLY
PAYMENT PERIODS	◯ WEEKLY ◯ MONTHLY	◯ 6-MO ◯ YEARLY
FEE AMOUNT		

SERVICES

- ◯ MOWING
- ◯ WEED EATING
- ◯ EDGING
- ◯ HEDGE TRIMMING
- ◯ WATERING

- ◯ FERTILIZING
- ◯ BLOWING
- ◯ MULCHING
- ◯ WEEDING
- ◯ LEAF/STRAW RAKING

- ◯ TREE TRIMMING PRUNING
- ◯ POWER WASHING
- ◯ PEST CONTROL
- ◯ GUTTER CLEANING
- ◯ AERATION

INSTRUCTIONS

TOOLS

INFORMATIONS

DATE: .... TIME: .... S M T W TH F S

CLIENT NAME	
PHONE NO	
EMAIL	
ADDRESS/ CITY-STATE-ZIP	

JOB FREQUENCY	WEEKLY /BI-WEEKLY	MONTHLY / BI-MONTHLY
PAYMENT PERIODS	○ WEEKLY ○ MONTHLY	○ 6-MO ○ YEARLY
FEE AMOUNT		

SERVICES

○ MOWING	○ FERTILIZING	○ TREE TRIMMING PRUNING
○ WEED EATING	○ BLOWING	○ POWER WASHING
○ EDGING	○ MULCHING	○ PEST CONTROL
○ HEDGE TRIMMING	○ WEEDING	○ GUTTER CLEANING
○ WATERING	○ LEAF/STRAW RAKING	○ AERATION

INSTRUCTIONS

TOOLS

INFORMATIONS

DATE: .... TIME: .... S M T W TH F S

CLIENT NAME	
PHONE NO	
EMAIL	
ADDRESS/ CITY-STATE-ZIP	

JOB FREQUENCY	WEEKLY /BI-WEEKLY	MONTHLY / BI-MONTHLY
PAYMENT PERIODS	○ WEEKLY ○ MONTHLY	○ 6-MO ○ YEARLY
FEE AMOUNT		

SERVICES

○ MOWING	○ FERTILIZING	○ TREE TRIMMING PRUNING
○ WEED EATING	○ BLOWING	○ POWER WASHING
○ EDGING	○ MULCHING	○ PEST CONTROL
○ HEDGE TRIMMING	○ WEEDING	○ GUTTER CLEANING
○ WATERING	○ LEAF/STRAW RAKING	○ AERATION

INSTRUCTIONS

TOOLS

INFORMATIONS

DATE: .... TIME: .... S M T W TH F S

CLIENT NAME	
PHONE NO	
EMAIL	
ADDRESS/ CITY-STATE-ZIP	

JOB FREQUENCY	WEEKLY /BI-WEEKLY	MONTHLY / BI-MONTHLY
PAYMENT PERIODS	○ WEEKLY ○ MONTHLY	○ 6-MO ○ YEARLY
FEE AMOUNT		

SERVICES

○ MOWING	○ FERTILIZING	○ TREE TRIMMING PRUNING
○ WEED EATING	○ BLOWING	○ POWER WASHING
○ EDGING	○ MULCHING	○ PEST CONTROL
○ HEDGE TRIMMING	○ WEEDING	○ GUTTER CLEANING
○ WATERING	○ LEAF/STRAW RAKING	○ AERATION

INSTRUCTIONS

TOOLS

INFORMATIONS

DATE: .... TIME: ....   S M T W TH F S

CLIENT NAME	
PHONE NO	
EMAIL	
ADDRESS/ CITY-STATE-ZIP	

JOB FREQUENCY	WEEKLY /BI-WEEKLY	MONTHLY / BI-MONTHLY
PAYMENT PERIODS	◯ WEEKLY ◯ MONTHLY	◯ 6-MO ◯ YEARLY
FEE AMOUNT		

SERVICES

◯ MOWING ◯ FERTILIZING ◯ TREE TRIMMING PRUNING

◯ WEED EATING ◯ BLOWING ◯ POWER WASHING

◯ EDGING ◯ MULCHING ◯ PEST CONTROL

◯ HEDGE TRIMMING ◯ WEEDING ◯ GUTTER CLEANING

◯ WATERING ◯ LEAF/STRAW RAKING ◯ AERATION

INSTRUCTIONS

TOOLS

INFORMATIONS

DATE: .... TIME: .... S M T W TH F S

CLIENT NAME	
PHONE NO	
EMAIL	
ADDRESS/ CITY-STATE-ZIP	

JOB FREQUENCY	WEEKLY /BI-WEEKLY	MONTHLY / BI-MONTHLY
PAYMENT PERIODS	○ WEEKLY ○ MONTHLY	○ 6-MO ○ YEARLY
FEE AMOUNT		

SERVICES

○ MOWING	○ FERTILIZING	○ TREE TRIMMING PRUNING
○ WEED EATING	○ BLOWING	○ POWER WASHING
○ EDGING	○ MULCHING	○ PEST CONTROL
○ HEDGE TRIMMING	○ WEEDING	○ GUTTER CLEANING
○ WATERING	○ LEAF/STRAW RAKING	○ AERATION

INSTRUCTIONS

TOOLS

INFORMATIONS

DATE: .... TIME: .... S M T W TH F S

CLIENT NAME	
PHONE NO	
EMAIL	
ADDRESS/ CITY-STATE-ZIP	

JOB FREQUENCY	WEEKLY /BI-WEEKLY	MONTHLY / BI-MONTHLY
PAYMENT PERIODS	○ WEEKLY ○ MONTHLY	○ 6-MO ○ YEARLY
FEE AMOUNT		

SERVICES

○ MOWING	○ FERTILIZING	○ TREE TRIMMING PRUNING
○ WEED EATING	○ BLOWING	○ POWER WASHING
○ EDGING	○ MULCHING	○ PEST CONTROL
○ HEDGE TRIMMING	○ WEEDING	○ GUTTER CLEANING
○ WATERING	○ LEAF/STRAW RAKING	○ AERATION

INSTRUCTIONS

TOOLS

INFORMATIONS

DATE: .... TIME: .... S M T W TH F S

CLIENT NAME	
PHONE NO	
EMAIL	
ADDRESS/ CITY-STATE-ZIP	

JOB FREQUENCY	WEEKLY /BI-WEEKLY	MONTHLY / BI-MONTHLY
PAYMENT PERIODS	○ WEEKLY ○ MONTHLY	○ 6-MO ○ YEARLY
FEE AMOUNT		

SERVICES

○ MOWING	○ FERTILIZING	○ TREE TRIMMING PRUNING
○ WEED EATING	○ BLOWING	○ POWER WASHING
○ EDGING	○ MULCHING	○ PEST CONTROL
○ HEDGE TRIMMING	○ WEEDING	○ GUTTER CLEANING
○ WATERING	○ LEAF/STRAW RAKING	○ AERATION

INSTRUCTIONS

TOOLS

INFORMATIONS

DATE: .... TIME: ....   S   M   T   W   TH   F   S

CLIENT NAME	
PHONE NO	
EMAIL	
ADDRESS/ CITY-STATE-ZIP	

JOB FREQUENCY	WEEKLY /BI-WEEKLY	MONTHLY / BI-MONTHLY
PAYMENT PERIODS	○ WEEKLY ○ MONTHLY	○ 6-MO ○ YEARLY
FEE AMOUNT		

SERVICES

○ MOWING	○ FERTILIZING	○ TREE TRIMMING PRUNING
○ WEED EATING	○ BLOWING	○ POWER WASHING
○ EDGING	○ MULCHING	○ PEST CONTROL
○ HEDGE TRIMMING	○ WEEDING	○ GUTTER CLEANING
○ WATERING	○ LEAF/STRAW RAKING	○ AERATION

INSTRUCTIONS

TOOLS

INFORMATIONS

DATE: .... TIME: .... S M T W TH F S

CLIENT NAME	
PHONE NO	
EMAIL	
ADDRESS/ CITY-STATE-ZIP	

JOB FREQUENCY	WEEKLY /BI-WEEKLY	MONTHLY / BI-MONTHLY
PAYMENT PERIODS	◯ WEEKLY ◯ MONTHLY	◯ 6-MO ◯ YEARLY
FEE AMOUNT		

SERVICES

◯ MOWING	◯ FERTILIZING	◯ TREE TRIMMING PRUNING
◯ WEED EATING	◯ BLOWING	◯ POWER WASHING
◯ EDGING	◯ MULCHING	◯ PEST CONTROL
◯ HEDGE TRIMMING	◯ WEEDING	◯ GUTTER CLEANING
◯ WATERING	◯ LEAF/STRAW RAKING	◯ AERATION

INSTRUCTIONS

TOOLS

INFORMATIONS

DATE: .... TIME: .... S M T W TH F S

CLIENT NAME	
PHONE NO	
EMAIL	
ADDRESS/ CITY-STATE-ZIP	

JOB FREQUENCY	WEEKLY /BI-WEEKLY	MONTHLY / BI-MONTHLY
PAYMENT PERIODS	○ WEEKLY ○ MONTHLY	○ 6-MO ○ YEARLY
FEE AMOUNT		

SERVICES

○ MOWING	○ FERTILIZING	○ TREE TRIMMING PRUNING
○ WEED EATING	○ BLOWING	○ POWER WASHING
○ EDGING	○ MULCHING	○ PEST CONTROL
○ HEDGE TRIMMING	○ WEEDING	○ GUTTER CLEANING
○ WATERING	○ LEAF/STRAW RAKING	○ AERATION

INSTRUCTIONS

TOOLS

INFORMATIONS

DATE: .... TIME: .... S M T W TH F S

CLIENT NAME	
PHONE NO	
EMAIL	
ADDRESS/ CITY-STATE-ZIP	

JOB FREQUENCY	WEEKLY /BI-WEEKLY	MONTHLY / BI-MONTHLY
PAYMENT PERIODS	○ WEEKLY ○ MONTHLY	○ 6-MO ○ YEARLY
FEE AMOUNT		

SERVICES

○ MOWING
○ WEED EATING
○ EDGING
○ HEDGE TRIMMING
○ WATERING

○ FERTILIZING
○ BLOWING
○ MULCHING
○ WEEDING
○ LEAF/STRAW RAKING

○ TREE TRIMMING PRUNING
○ POWER WASHING
○ PEST CONTROL
○ GUTTER CLEANING
○ AERATION

INSTRUCTIONS

TOOLS

INFORMATIONS

DATE: .... TIME: .... S M T W TH F S

CLIENT NAME	
PHONE NO	
EMAIL	
ADDRESS/ CITY-STATE-ZIP	

JOB FREQUENCY	WEEKLY /BI-WEEKLY	MONTHLY / BI-MONTHLY
PAYMENT PERIODS	○ WEEKLY ○ MONTHLY	○ 6-MO ○ YEARLY
FEE AMOUNT		

SERVICES

○ MOWING	○ FERTILIZING	○ TREE TRIMMING PRUNING
○ WEED EATING	○ BLOWING	○ POWER WASHING
○ EDGING	○ MULCHING	○ PEST CONTROL
○ HEDGE TRIMMING	○ WEEDING	○ GUTTER CLEANING
○ WATERING	○ LEAF/STRAW RAKING	○ AERATION

INSTRUCTIONS

TOOLS

INFORMATIONS

DATE: .... TIME: .... S M T W TH F S

CLIENT NAME	
PHONE NO	
EMAIL	
ADDRESS/ CITY-STATE-ZIP	

JOB FREQUENCY	WEEKLY /BI-WEEKLY	MONTHLY / BI-MONTHLY
PAYMENT PERIODS	○ WEEKLY ○ MONTHLY	○ 6-MO ○ YEARLY
FEE AMOUNT		

SERVICES

○ MOWING	○ FERTILIZING	○ TREE TRIMMING PRUNING
○ WEED EATING	○ BLOWING	○ POWER WASHING
○ EDGING	○ MULCHING	○ PEST CONTROL
○ HEDGE TRIMMING	○ WEEDING	○ GUTTER CLEANING
○ WATERING	○ LEAF/STRAW RAKING	○ AERATION

INSTRUCTIONS

TOOLS

INFORMATIONS

DATE: .... TIME: .... S M T W TH F S

CLIENT NAME	
PHONE NO	
EMAIL	
ADDRESS/ CITY-STATE-ZIP	

JOB FREQUENCY	WEEKLY /BI-WEEKLY	MONTHLY / BI-MONTHLY
PAYMENT PERIODS	○ WEEKLY ○ MONTHLY	○ 6-MO ○ YEARLY
FEE AMOUNT		

SERVICES

- ○ MOWING
- ○ WEED EATING
- ○ EDGING
- ○ HEDGE TRIMMING
- ○ WATERING

- ○ FERTILIZING
- ○ BLOWING
- ○ MULCHING
- ○ WEEDING
- ○ LEAF/STRAW RAKING

- ○ TREE TRIMMING PRUNING
- ○ POWER WASHING
- ○ PEST CONTROL
- ○ GUTTER CLEANING
- ○ AERATION

INSTRUCTIONS

TOOLS

INFORMATIONS

DATE: .... TIME: .... S M T W TH F S

CLIENT NAME	
PHONE NO	
EMAIL	
ADDRESS/ CITY-STATE-ZIP	

JOB FREQUENCY	WEEKLY /BI-WEEKLY	MONTHLY / BI-MONTHLY
PAYMENT PERIODS	○ WEEKLY ○ MONTHLY	○ 6-MO ○ YEARLY
FEE AMOUNT		

SERVICES

○ MOWING	○ FERTILIZING	○ TREE TRIMMING PRUNING
○ WEED EATING	○ BLOWING	○ POWER WASHING
○ EDGING	○ MULCHING	○ PEST CONTROL
○ HEDGE TRIMMING	○ WEEDING	○ GUTTER CLEANING
○ WATERING	○ LEAF/STRAW RAKING	○ AERATION

INSTRUCTIONS

TOOLS

INFORMATIONS

DATE: .... TIME: .... S M T W TH F S

CLIENT NAME	
PHONE NO	
EMAIL	
ADDRESS/ CITY-STATE-ZIP	

JOB FREQUENCY	WEEKLY /BI-WEEKLY	MONTHLY / BI-MONTHLY
PAYMENT PERIODS	◯ WEEKLY ◯ MONTHLY	◯ 6-MO ◯ YEARLY
FEE AMOUNT		

SERVICES

◯ MOWING	◯ FERTILIZING	◯ TREE TRIMMING PRUNING
◯ WEED EATING	◯ BLOWING	◯ POWER WASHING
◯ EDGING	◯ MULCHING	◯ PEST CONTROL
◯ HEDGE TRIMMING	◯ WEEDING	◯ GUTTER CLEANING
◯ WATERING	◯ LEAF/STRAW RAKING	◯ AERATION

INSTRUCTIONS

TOOLS

INFORMATIONS

DATE: .... TIME: ....   S M T W TH F S

CLIENT NAME	
PHONE NO	
EMAIL	
ADDRESS/ CITY-STATE-ZIP	

JOB FREQUENCY	WEEKLY /BI-WEEKLY	MONTHLY / BI-MONTHLY
PAYMENT PERIODS	○ WEEKLY ○ MONTHLY	○ 6-MO ○ YEARLY
FEE AMOUNT		

SERVICES

○ MOWING	○ FERTILIZING	○ TREE TRIMMING PRUNING
○ WEED EATING	○ BLOWING	○ POWER WASHING
○ EDGING	○ MULCHING	○ PEST CONTROL
○ HEDGE TRIMMING	○ WEEDING	○ GUTTER CLEANING
○ WATERING	○ LEAF/STRAW RAKING	○ AERATION

INSTRUCTIONS

TOOLS

INFORMATIONS

DATE: .... TIME: .... S M T W TH F S

CLIENT NAME	
PHONE NO	
EMAIL	
ADDRESS/ CITY-STATE-ZIP	

JOB FREQUENCY	WEEKLY /BI-WEEKLY	MONTHLY / BI-MONTHLY
PAYMENT PERIODS	○ WEEKLY ○ MONTHLY	○ 6-MO ○ YEARLY
FEE AMOUNT		

SERVICES

○ MOWING	○ FERTILIZING	○ TREE TRIMMING PRUNING
○ WEED EATING	○ BLOWING	○ POWER WASHING
○ EDGING	○ MULCHING	○ PEST CONTROL
○ HEDGE TRIMMING	○ WEEDING	○ GUTTER CLEANING
○ WATERING	○ LEAF/STRAW RAKING	○ AERATION

INSTRUCTIONS

TOOLS

DATE: .... TIME: .... S M T W TH F S

CLIENT NAME	
PHONE NO	
EMAIL	
ADDRESS/ CITY-STATE-ZIP	

JOB FREQUENCY	WEEKLY /BI-WEEKLY	MONTHLY / BI-MONTHLY
PAYMENT PERIODS	◯ WEEKLY ◯ MONTHLY	◯ 6-MO ◯ YEARLY
FEE AMOUNT		

SERVICES

◯ MOWING	◯ FERTILIZING	◯ TREE TRIMMING PRUNING
◯ WEED EATING	◯ BLOWING	◯ POWER WASHING
◯ EDGING	◯ MULCHING	◯ PEST CONTROL
◯ HEDGE TRIMMING	◯ WEEDING	◯ GUTTER CLEANING
◯ WATERING	◯ LEAF/STRAW RAKING	◯ AERATION

INSTRUCTIONS

TOOLS

INFORMATIONS

DATE: .... TIME: .... S M T W TH F S

CLIENT NAME	
PHONE NO	
EMAIL	
ADDRESS/ CITY-STATE-ZIP	

JOB FREQUENCY	WEEKLY /BI-WEEKLY	MONTHLY / BI-MONTHLY
PAYMENT PERIODS	○ WEEKLY ○ MONTHLY	○ 6-MO ○ YEARLY
FEE AMOUNT		

SERVICES

○ MOWING	○ FERTILIZING	○ TREE TRIMMING PRUNING
○ WEED EATING	○ BLOWING	○ POWER WASHING
○ EDGING	○ MULCHING	○ PEST CONTROL
○ HEDGE TRIMMING	○ WEEDING	○ GUTTER CLEANING
○ WATERING	○ LEAF/STRAW RAKING	○ AERATION

INSTRUCTIONS

TOOLS

INFORMATIONS

DATE: .... TIME: .... S M T W TH F S

CLIENT NAME	
PHONE NO	
EMAIL	
ADDRESS/ CITY-STATE-ZIP	

JOB FREQUENCY	WEEKLY /BI-WEEKLY	MONTHLY / BI-MONTHLY
PAYMENT PERIODS	○ WEEKLY ○ MONTHLY	○ 6-MO ○ YEARLY
FEE AMOUNT		

SERVICES

○ MOWING	○ FERTILIZING	○ TREE TRIMMING PRUNING
○ WEED EATING	○ BLOWING	○ POWER WASHING
○ EDGING	○ MULCHING	○ PEST CONTROL
○ HEDGE TRIMMING	○ WEEDING	○ GUTTER CLEANING
○ WATERING	○ LEAF/STRAW RAKING	○ AERATION

INSTRUCTIONS

TOOLS

INFORMATIONS

DATE: .... TIME: .... S M T W TH F S

CLIENT NAME	
PHONE NO	
EMAIL	
ADDRESS/ CITY-STATE-ZIP	

JOB FREQUENCY	WEEKLY /BI-WEEKLY	MONTHLY / BI-MONTHLY
PAYMENT PERIODS	○ WEEKLY ○ MONTHLY	○ 6-MO ○ YEARLY
FEE AMOUNT		

SERVICES

○ MOWING   ○ FERTILIZING   ○ TREE TRIMMING PRUNING
○ WEED EATING   ○ BLOWING   ○ POWER WASHING
○ EDGING   ○ MULCHING   ○ PEST CONTROL
○ HEDGE TRIMMING   ○ WEEDING   ○ GUTTER CLEANING
○ WATERING   ○ LEAF/STRAW RAKING   ○ AERATION

INSTRUCTIONS

TOOLS

INFORMATIONS

DATE: .... TIME: ....   S   M   T   W   TH   F   S

CLIENT NAME	
PHONE NO	
EMAIL	
ADDRESS/ CITY-STATE-ZIP	

JOB FREQUENCY	WEEKLY /BI-WEEKLY	MONTHLY / BI-MONTHLY
PAYMENT PERIODS	○ WEEKLY ○ MONTHLY	○ 6-MO ○ YEARLY
FEE AMOUNT		

SERVICES

○ MOWING	○ FERTILIZING	○ TREE TRIMMING PRUNING
○ WEED EATING	○ BLOWING	○ POWER WASHING
○ EDGING	○ MULCHING	○ PEST CONTROL
○ HEDGE TRIMMING	○ WEEDING	○ GUTTER CLEANING
○ WATERING	○ LEAF/STRAW RAKING	○ AERATION

INSTRUCTIONS

TOOLS

INFORMATIONS

DATE: .... TIME: .... S M T W TH F S

CLIENT NAME	
PHONE NO	
EMAIL	
ADDRESS/ CITY-STATE-ZIP	

JOB FREQUENCY	WEEKLY /BI-WEEKLY	MONTHLY / BI-MONTHLY
PAYMENT PERIODS	○ WEEKLY ○ MONTHLY	○ 6-MO ○ YEARLY
FEE AMOUNT		

SERVICES

○ MOWING	○ FERTILIZING	○ TREE TRIMMING PRUNING
○ WEED EATING	○ BLOWING	○ POWER WASHING
○ EDGING	○ MULCHING	○ PEST CONTROL
○ HEDGE TRIMMING	○ WEEDING	○ GUTTER CLEANING
○ WATERING	○ LEAF/STRAW RAKING	○ AERATION

INSTRUCTIONS

TOOLS

INFORMATIONS

DATE: .... TIME: .... S M T W TH F S

CLIENT NAME	
PHONE NO	
EMAIL	
ADDRESS/ CITY-STATE-ZIP	

JOB FREQUENCY	WEEKLY /BI-WEEKLY	MONTHLY / BI-MONTHLY
PAYMENT PERIODS	○ WEEKLY ○ MONTHLY	○ 6-MO ○ YEARLY
FEE AMOUNT		

SERVICES

○ MOWING	○ FERTILIZING	○ TREE TRIMMING PRUNING
○ WEED EATING	○ BLOWING	○ POWER WASHING
○ EDGING	○ MULCHING	○ PEST CONTROL
○ HEDGE TRIMMING	○ WEEDING	○ GUTTER CLEANING
○ WATERING	○ LEAF/STRAW RAKING	○ AERATION

INSTRUCTIONS

TOOLS

INFORMATIONS

DATE: .... TIME: ....   S M T W TH F S

CLIENT NAME	
PHONE NO	
EMAIL	
ADDRESS/ CITY-STATE-ZIP	

JOB FREQUENCY	WEEKLY /BI-WEEKLY	MONTHLY / BI-MONTHLY
PAYMENT PERIODS	○ WEEKLY ○ MONTHLY	○ 6-MO ○ YEARLY
FEE AMOUNT		

SERVICES

○ MOWING	○ FERTILIZING	○ TREE TRIMMING PRUNING
○ WEED EATING	○ BLOWING	○ POWER WASHING
○ EDGING	○ MULCHING	○ PEST CONTROL
○ HEDGE TRIMMING	○ WEEDING	○ GUTTER CLEANING
○ WATERING	○ LEAF/STRAW RAKING	○ AERATION

INSTRUCTIONS

TOOLS

INFORMATIONS

DATE: .... TIME: .... S M T W TH F S

CLIENT NAME	
PHONE NO	
EMAIL	
ADDRESS/ CITY-STATE-ZIP	

JOB FREQUENCY	WEEKLY /BI-WEEKLY	MONTHLY / BI-MONTHLY
PAYMENT PERIODS	○ WEEKLY ○ MONTHLY	○ 6-MO ○ YEARLY
FEE AMOUNT		

SERVICES

○ MOWING	○ FERTILIZING	○ TREE TRIMMING PRUNING
○ WEED EATING	○ BLOWING	○ POWER WASHING
○ EDGING	○ MULCHING	○ PEST CONTROL
○ HEDGE TRIMMING	○ WEEDING	○ GUTTER CLEANING
○ WATERING	○ LEAF/STRAW RAKING	○ AERATION

INSTRUCTIONS

TOOLS

INFORMATIONS

DATE: .... TIME: .... S M T W TH F S

CLIENT NAME	
PHONE NO	
EMAIL	
ADDRESS/ CITY-STATE-ZIP	

JOB FREQUENCY	WEEKLY /BI-WEEKLY	MONTHLY / BI-MONTHLY
PAYMENT PERIODS	◯ WEEKLY ◯ MONTHLY	◯ 6-MO ◯ YEARLY
FEE AMOUNT		

SERVICES

◯ MOWING	◯ FERTILIZING	◯ TREE TRIMMING PRUNING
◯ WEED EATING	◯ BLOWING	◯ POWER WASHING
◯ EDGING	◯ MULCHING	◯ PEST CONTROL
◯ HEDGE TRIMMING	◯ WEEDING	◯ GUTTER CLEANING
◯ WATERING	◯ LEAF/STRAW RAKING	◯ AERATION

INSTRUCTIONS

TOOLS

INFORMATIONS

DATE: .... TIME: .... S M T W TH F S

CLIENT NAME	
PHONE NO	
EMAIL	
ADDRESS/ CITY-STATE-ZIP	

JOB FREQUENCY	WEEKLY /BI-WEEKLY	MONTHLY / BI-MONTHLY
PAYMENT PERIODS	○ WEEKLY ○ MONTHLY	○ 6-MO ○ YEARLY
FEE AMOUNT		

SERVICES

○ MOWING	○ FERTILIZING	○ TREE TRIMMING PRUNING
○ WEED EATING	○ BLOWING	○ POWER WASHING
○ EDGING	○ MULCHING	○ PEST CONTROL
○ HEDGE TRIMMING	○ WEEDING	○ GUTTER CLEANING
○ WATERING	○ LEAF/STRAW RAKING	○ AERATION

INSTRUCTIONS

TOOLS

INFORMATIONS

DATE: .... TIME: .... S M T W TH F S

CLIENT NAME	
PHONE NO	
EMAIL	
ADDRESS/ CITY-STATE-ZIP	

JOB FREQUENCY	WEEKLY /BI-WEEKLY	MONTHLY / BI-MONTHLY
PAYMENT PERIODS	○ WEEKLY ○ MONTHLY	○ 6-MO ○ YEARLY
FEE AMOUNT		

SERVICES

○ MOWING	○ FERTILIZING	○ TREE TRIMMING PRUNING
○ WEED EATING	○ BLOWING	○ POWER WASHING
○ EDGING	○ MULCHING	○ PEST CONTROL
○ HEDGE TRIMMING	○ WEEDING	○ GUTTER CLEANING
○ WATERING	○ LEAF/STRAW RAKING	○ AERATION

INSTRUCTIONS

TOOLS

INFORMATIONS

DATE: .... TIME: .... S M T W TH F S

CLIENT NAME	
PHONE NO	
EMAIL	
ADDRESS/ CITY-STATE-ZIP	

JOB FREQUENCY	WEEKLY /BI-WEEKLY	MONTHLY / BI-MONTHLY
PAYMENT PERIODS	◯ WEEKLY ◯ MONTHLY	◯ 6-MO ◯ YEARLY
FEE AMOUNT		

SERVICES

◯ MOWING	◯ FERTILIZING	◯ TREE TRIMMING PRUNING
◯ WEED EATING	◯ BLOWING	◯ POWER WASHING
◯ EDGING	◯ MULCHING	◯ PEST CONTROL
◯ HEDGE TRIMMING	◯ WEEDING	◯ GUTTER CLEANING
◯ WATERING	◯ LEAF/STRAW RAKING	◯ AERATION

INSTRUCTIONS

TOOLS

INFORMATIONS

DATE: .... TIME: .... S M T W TH F S

CLIENT NAME	
PHONE NO	
EMAIL	
ADDRESS/ CITY-STATE-ZIP	

JOB FREQUENCY	WEEKLY /BI-WEEKLY	MONTHLY / BI-MONTHLY
PAYMENT PERIODS	○ WEEKLY ○ MONTHLY	○ 6-MO ○ YEARLY
FEE AMOUNT		

SERVICES

○ MOWING	○ FERTILIZING	○ TREE TRIMMING PRUNING
○ WEED EATING	○ BLOWING	○ POWER WASHING
○ EDGING	○ MULCHING	○ PEST CONTROL
○ HEDGE TRIMMING	○ WEEDING	○ GUTTER CLEANING
○ WATERING	○ LEAF/STRAW RAKING	○ AERATION

INSTRUCTIONS

TOOLS

INFORMATIONS

DATE: .... TIME: .... S M T W TH F S

CLIENT NAME	
PHONE NO	
EMAIL	
ADDRESS/ CITY-STATE-ZIP	

JOB FREQUENCY	WEEKLY /BI-WEEKLY	MONTHLY / BI-MONTHLY
PAYMENT PERIODS	○ WEEKLY ○ MONTHLY	○ 6-MO ○ YEARLY
FEE AMOUNT		

SERVICES

○ MOWING	○ FERTILIZING	○ TREE TRIMMING PRUNING
○ WEED EATING	○ BLOWING	○ POWER WASHING
○ EDGING	○ MULCHING	○ PEST CONTROL
○ HEDGE TRIMMING	○ WEEDING	○ GUTTER CLEANING
○ WATERING	○ LEAF/STRAW RAKING	○ AERATION

INSTRUCTIONS

TOOLS

INFORMATIONS

DATE: .... TIME: .... S M T W TH F S

CLIENT NAME	
PHONE NO	
EMAIL	
ADDRESS/ CITY-STATE-ZIP	

JOB FREQUENCY	WEEKLY /BI-WEEKLY	MONTHLY / BI-MONTHLY
PAYMENT PERIODS	○ WEEKLY ○ MONTHLY	○ 6-MO ○ YEARLY
FEE AMOUNT		

SERVICES

○ MOWING	○ FERTILIZING	○ TREE TRIMMING PRUNING
○ WEED EATING	○ BLOWING	○ POWER WASHING
○ EDGING	○ MULCHING	○ PEST CONTROL
○ HEDGE TRIMMING	○ WEEDING	○ GUTTER CLEANING
○ WATERING	○ LEAF/STRAW RAKING	○ AERATION

INSTRUCTIONS

TOOLS

INFORMATIONS

DATE: .... TIME: .... S M T W TH F S

CLIENT NAME	
PHONE NO	
EMAIL	
ADDRESS/ CITY-STATE-ZIP	

JOB FREQUENCY	WEEKLY /BI-WEEKLY	MONTHLY / BI-MONTHLY
PAYMENT PERIODS	○ WEEKLY ○ MONTHLY	○ 6-MO ○ YEARLY
FEE AMOUNT		

SERVICES

○ MOWING	○ FERTILIZING	○ TREE TRIMMING PRUNING
○ WEED EATING	○ BLOWING	○ POWER WASHING
○ EDGING	○ MULCHING	○ PEST CONTROL
○ HEDGE TRIMMING	○ WEEDING	○ GUTTER CLEANING
○ WATERING	○ LEAF/STRAW RAKING	○ AERATION

INSTRUCTIONS

TOOLS

INFORMATIONS

DATE: .... TIME: .... S M T W TH F S

CLIENT NAME	
PHONE NO	
EMAIL	
ADDRESS/ CITY-STATE-ZIP	

JOB FREQUENCY	WEEKLY /BI-WEEKLY	MONTHLY / BI-MONTHLY
PAYMENT PERIODS	○ WEEKLY ○ MONTHLY	○ 6-MO ○ YEARLY
FEE AMOUNT		

SERVICES

○ MOWING	○ FERTILIZING	○ TREE TRIMMING PRUNING
○ WEED EATING	○ BLOWING	○ POWER WASHING
○ EDGING	○ MULCHING	○ PEST CONTROL
○ HEDGE TRIMMING	○ WEEDING	○ GUTTER CLEANING
○ WATERING	○ LEAF/STRAW RAKING	○ AERATION

INSTRUCTIONS

TOOLS

INFORMATIONS

DATE: .... TIME: .... S M T W TH F S

CLIENT NAME	
PHONE NO	
EMAIL	
ADDRESS/ CITY-STATE-ZIP	

JOB FREQUENCY	WEEKLY /BI-WEEKLY	MONTHLY / BI-MONTHLY
PAYMENT PERIODS	○ WEEKLY ○ MONTHLY	○ 6-MO ○ YEARLY
FEE AMOUNT		

SERVICES

○ MOWING	○ FERTILIZING	○ TREE TRIMMING PRUNING
○ WEED EATING	○ BLOWING	○ POWER WASHING
○ EDGING	○ MULCHING	○ PEST CONTROL
○ HEDGE TRIMMING	○ WEEDING	○ GUTTER CLEANING
○ WATERING	○ LEAF/STRAW RAKING	○ AERATION

INSTRUCTIONS

TOOLS

INFORMATIONS

DATE: .... TIME: .... S M T W TH F S

CLIENT NAME	
PHONE NO	
EMAIL	
ADDRESS/ CITY-STATE-ZIP	

JOB FREQUENCY	WEEKLY /BI-WEEKLY	MONTHLY / BI-MONTHLY
PAYMENT PERIODS	○ WEEKLY ○ MONTHLY	○ 6-MO ○ YEARLY
FEE AMOUNT		

SERVICES

○ MOWING	○ FERTILIZING	○ TREE TRIMMING PRUNING
○ WEED EATING	○ BLOWING	○ POWER WASHING
○ EDGING	○ MULCHING	○ PEST CONTROL
○ HEDGE TRIMMING	○ WEEDING	○ GUTTER CLEANING
○ WATERING	○ LEAF/STRAW RAKING	○ AERATION

INSTRUCTIONS

TOOLS

INFORMATIONS

DATE: .... TIME: .... S M T W TH F S

CLIENT NAME	
PHONE NO	
EMAIL	
ADDRESS/ CITY-STATE-ZIP	

JOB FREQUENCY	WEEKLY /BI-WEEKLY	MONTHLY / BI-MONTHLY
PAYMENT PERIODS	○ WEEKLY ○ MONTHLY	○ 6-MO ○ YEARLY
FEE AMOUNT		

SERVICES

○ MOWING	○ FERTILIZING	○ TREE TRIMMING PRUNING
○ WEED EATING	○ BLOWING	○ POWER WASHING
○ EDGING	○ MULCHING	○ PEST CONTROL
○ HEDGE TRIMMING	○ WEEDING	○ GUTTER CLEANING
○ WATERING	○ LEAF/STRAW RAKING	○ AERATION

INSTRUCTIONS

TOOLS

INFORMATIONS

DATE: .... TIME: .... S M T W TH F S

CLIENT NAME	
PHONE NO	
EMAIL	
ADDRESS/ CITY-STATE-ZIP	

JOB FREQUENCY	WEEKLY /BI-WEEKLY	MONTHLY / BI-MONTHLY
PAYMENT PERIODS	○ WEEKLY ○ MONTHLY	○ 6-MO ○ YEARLY
FEE AMOUNT		

SERVICES

- ○ MOWING
- ○ WEED EATING
- ○ EDGING
- ○ HEDGE TRIMMING
- ○ WATERING

- ○ FERTILIZING
- ○ BLOWING
- ○ MULCHING
- ○ WEEDING
- ○ LEAF/STRAW RAKING

- ○ TREE TRIMMING PRUNING
- ○ POWER WASHING
- ○ PEST CONTROL
- ○ GUTTER CLEANING
- ○ AERATION

INSTRUCTIONS

TOOLS

DATE: .... TIME: .... S M T W TH F S

CLIENT NAME	
PHONE NO	
EMAIL	
ADDRESS/ CITY-STATE-ZIP	

JOB FREQUENCY	WEEKLY /BI-WEEKLY	MONTHLY / BI-MONTHLY
PAYMENT PERIODS	○ WEEKLY ○ MONTHLY	○ 6-MO ○ YEARLY
FEE AMOUNT		

SERVICES

○ MOWING	○ FERTILIZING	○ TREE TRIMMING PRUNING
○ WEED EATING	○ BLOWING	○ POWER WASHING
○ EDGING	○ MULCHING	○ PEST CONTROL
○ HEDGE TRIMMING	○ WEEDING	○ GUTTER CLEANING
○ WATERING	○ LEAF/STRAW RAKING	○ AERATION

INSTRUCTIONS

TOOLS

INFORMATIONS

DATE: .... TIME: .... S M T W TH F S

CLIENT NAME	
PHONE NO	
EMAIL	
ADDRESS/ CITY-STATE-ZIP	

JOB FREQUENCY	WEEKLY /BI-WEEKLY	MONTHLY / BI-MONTHLY
PAYMENT PERIODS	○ WEEKLY ○ MONTHLY	○ 6-MO ○ YEARLY
FEE AMOUNT		

SERVICES

- ○ MOWING
- ○ WEED EATING
- ○ EDGING
- ○ HEDGE TRIMMING
- ○ WATERING

- ○ FERTILIZING
- ○ BLOWING
- ○ MULCHING
- ○ WEEDING
- ○ LEAF/STRAW RAKING

- ○ TREE TRIMMING PRUNING
- ○ POWER WASHING
- ○ PEST CONTROL
- ○ GUTTER CLEANING
- ○ AERATION

INSTRUCTIONS

TOOLS

INFORMATIONS

DATE: .... TIME: ....   S M T W TH F S

CLIENT NAME	
PHONE NO	
EMAIL	
ADDRESS/ CITY-STATE-ZIP	

JOB FREQUENCY	WEEKLY /BI-WEEKLY	MONTHLY / BI-MONTHLY
PAYMENT PERIODS	○ WEEKLY ○ MONTHLY	○ 6-MO ○ YEARLY
FEE AMOUNT		

SERVICES

○ MOWING	○ FERTILIZING	○ TREE TRIMMING PRUNING
○ WEED EATING	○ BLOWING	○ POWER WASHING
○ EDGING	○ MULCHING	○ PEST CONTROL
○ HEDGE TRIMMING	○ WEEDING	○ GUTTER CLEANING
○ WATERING	○ LEAF/STRAW RAKING	○ AERATION

INSTRUCTIONS

TOOLS

INFORMATIONS

DATE: .... TIME: .... S M T W TH F S

CLIENT NAME	
PHONE NO	
EMAIL	
ADDRESS/ CITY-STATE-ZIP	

JOB FREQUENCY	WEEKLY /BI-WEEKLY	MONTHLY / BI-MONTHLY
PAYMENT PERIODS	○ WEEKLY ○ MONTHLY	○ 6-MO ○ YEARLY
FEE AMOUNT		

SERVICES

○ MOWING	○ FERTILIZING	○ TREE TRIMMING PRUNING
○ WEED EATING	○ BLOWING	○ POWER WASHING
○ EDGING	○ MULCHING	○ PEST CONTROL
○ HEDGE TRIMMING	○ WEEDING	○ GUTTER CLEANING
○ WATERING	○ LEAF/STRAW RAKING	○ AERATION

INSTRUCTIONS

TOOLS

INFORMATIONS

DATE: .... TIME: ....   S M T W TH F S

CLIENT NAME	
PHONE NO	
EMAIL	
ADDRESS/ CITY-STATE-ZIP	

JOB FREQUENCY	WEEKLY /BI-WEEKLY	MONTHLY / BI-MONTHLY
PAYMENT PERIODS	○ WEEKLY ○ MONTHLY	○ 6-MO ○ YEARLY
FEE AMOUNT		

SERVICES

○ MOWING	○ FERTILIZING	○ TREE TRIMMING PRUNING
○ WEED EATING	○ BLOWING	○ POWER WASHING
○ EDGING	○ MULCHING	○ PEST CONTROL
○ HEDGE TRIMMING	○ WEEDING	○ GUTTER CLEANING
○ WATERING	○ LEAF/STRAW RAKING	○ AERATION

INSTRUCTIONS

TOOLS

INFORMATIONS

DATE: .... TIME: .... S M T W TH F S

CLIENT NAME	
PHONE NO	
EMAIL	
ADDRESS/ CITY-STATE-ZIP	

JOB FREQUENCY	WEEKLY /BI-WEEKLY	MONTHLY / BI-MONTHLY
PAYMENT PERIODS	◯ WEEKLY ◯ MONTHLY	◯ 6-MO ◯ YEARLY
FEE AMOUNT		

SERVICES

◯ MOWING	◯ FERTILIZING	◯ TREE TRIMMING PRUNING
◯ WEED EATING	◯ BLOWING	◯ POWER WASHING
◯ EDGING	◯ MULCHING	◯ PEST CONTROL
◯ HEDGE TRIMMING	◯ WEEDING	◯ GUTTER CLEANING
◯ WATERING	◯ LEAF/STRAW RAKING	◯ AERATION

INSTRUCTIONS

TOOLS

INFORMATIONS

DATE: .... TIME: .... S M T W TH F S

CLIENT NAME	
PHONE NO	
EMAIL	
ADDRESS/ CITY-STATE-ZIP	

JOB FREQUENCY	WEEKLY /BI-WEEKLY	MONTHLY / BI-MONTHLY
PAYMENT PERIODS	○ WEEKLY ○ MONTHLY	○ 6-MO ○ YEARLY
FEE AMOUNT		

SERVICES

○ MOWING	○ FERTILIZING	○ TREE TRIMMING PRUNING
○ WEED EATING	○ BLOWING	○ POWER WASHING
○ EDGING	○ MULCHING	○ PEST CONTROL
○ HEDGE TRIMMING	○ WEEDING	○ GUTTER CLEANING
○ WATERING	○ LEAF/STRAW RAKING	○ AERATION

INSTRUCTIONS

TOOLS

INFORMATIONS

DATE: .... TIME: .... S M T W TH F S

CLIENT NAME	
PHONE NO	
EMAIL	
ADDRESS/ CITY-STATE-ZIP	

JOB FREQUENCY	WEEKLY /BI-WEEKLY	MONTHLY / BI-MONTHLY
PAYMENT PERIODS	◯ WEEKLY ◯ MONTHLY	◯ 6-MO ◯ YEARLY
FEE AMOUNT		

SERVICES

- ◯ MOWING
- ◯ WEED EATING
- ◯ EDGING
- ◯ HEDGE TRIMMING
- ◯ WATERING

- ◯ FERTILIZING
- ◯ BLOWING
- ◯ MULCHING
- ◯ WEEDING
- ◯ LEAF/STRAW RAKING

- ◯ TREE TRIMMING PRUNING
- ◯ POWER WASHING
- ◯ PEST CONTROL
- ◯ GUTTER CLEANING
- ◯ AERATION

INSTRUCTIONS

TOOLS

INFORMATIONS

DATE: .... TIME: .... S M T W TH F S

CLIENT NAME	
PHONE NO	
EMAIL	
ADDRESS/ CITY-STATE-ZIP	

JOB FREQUENCY	WEEKLY /BI-WEEKLY	MONTHLY / BI-MONTHLY
PAYMENT PERIODS	○ WEEKLY ○ MONTHLY	○ 6-MO ○ YEARLY
FEE AMOUNT		

SERVICES

○ MOWING	○ FERTILIZING	○ TREE TRIMMING PRUNING
○ WEED EATING	○ BLOWING	○ POWER WASHING
○ EDGING	○ MULCHING	○ PEST CONTROL
○ HEDGE TRIMMING	○ WEEDING	○ GUTTER CLEANING
○ WATERING	○ LEAF/STRAW RAKING	○ AERATION

INSTRUCTIONS

TOOLS

INFORMATIONS

DATE: .... TIME: .... S M T W TH F S

CLIENT NAME	
PHONE NO	
EMAIL	
ADDRESS/ CITY-STATE-ZIP	

JOB FREQUENCY	WEEKLY /BI-WEEKLY	MONTHLY / BI-MONTHLY
PAYMENT PERIODS	○ WEEKLY ○ MONTHLY	○ 6-MO ○ YEARLY
FEE AMOUNT		

SERVICES

○ MOWING	○ FERTILIZING	○ TREE TRIMMING PRUNING
○ WEED EATING	○ BLOWING	○ POWER WASHING
○ EDGING	○ MULCHING	○ PEST CONTROL
○ HEDGE TRIMMING	○ WEEDING	○ GUTTER CLEANING
○ WATERING	○ LEAF/STRAW RAKING	○ AERATION

INSTRUCTIONS

TOOLS

INFORMATIONS

DATE: .... TIME: .... S M T W TH F S

CLIENT NAME	
PHONE NO	
EMAIL	
ADDRESS/ CITY-STATE-ZIP	

JOB FREQUENCY	WEEKLY /BI-WEEKLY	MONTHLY / BI-MONTHLY
PAYMENT PERIODS	○ WEEKLY ○ MONTHLY	○ 6-MO ○ YEARLY
FEE AMOUNT		

SERVICES

○ MOWING	○ FERTILIZING	○ TREE TRIMMING PRUNING
○ WEED EATING	○ BLOWING	○ POWER WASHING
○ EDGING	○ MULCHING	○ PEST CONTROL
○ HEDGE TRIMMING	○ WEEDING	○ GUTTER CLEANING
○ WATERING	○ LEAF/STRAW RAKING	○ AERATION

INSTRUCTIONS

TOOLS

INFORMATIONS

DATE: .... TIME: .... S M T W TH F S

CLIENT NAME	
PHONE NO	
EMAIL	
ADDRESS/ CITY-STATE-ZIP	

JOB FREQUENCY	WEEKLY /BI-WEEKLY	MONTHLY / BI-MONTHLY
PAYMENT PERIODS	○ WEEKLY ○ MONTHLY	○ 6-MO ○ YEARLY
FEE AMOUNT		

SERVICES

○ MOWING	○ FERTILIZING	○ TREE TRIMMING PRUNING
○ WEED EATING	○ BLOWING	○ POWER WASHING
○ EDGING	○ MULCHING	○ PEST CONTROL
○ HEDGE TRIMMING	○ WEEDING	○ GUTTER CLEANING
○ WATERING	○ LEAF/STRAW RAKING	○ AERATION

INSTRUCTIONS

TOOLS

DATE: .... TIME: .... S M T W TH F S

CLIENT NAME	
PHONE NO	
EMAIL	
ADDRESS/ CITY-STATE-ZIP	

JOB FREQUENCY	WEEKLY /BI-WEEKLY	MONTHLY / BI-MONTHLY
PAYMENT PERIODS	○ WEEKLY ○ MONTHLY	○ 6-MO ○ YEARLY
FEE AMOUNT		

SERVICES

○ MOWING	○ FERTILIZING	○ TREE TRIMMING PRUNING
○ WEED EATING	○ BLOWING	○ POWER WASHING
○ EDGING	○ MULCHING	○ PEST CONTROL
○ HEDGE TRIMMING	○ WEEDING	○ GUTTER CLEANING
○ WATERING	○ LEAF/STRAW RAKING	○ AERATION

INSTRUCTIONS

TOOLS

INFORMATIONS

DATE: .... TIME: .... S M T W TH F S

CLIENT NAME	
PHONE NO	
EMAIL	
ADDRESS/ CITY-STATE-ZIP	

JOB FREQUENCY	WEEKLY /BI-WEEKLY	MONTHLY / BI-MONTHLY
PAYMENT PERIODS	○ WEEKLY ○ MONTHLY	○ 6-MO ○ YEARLY
FEE AMOUNT		

SERVICES

○ MOWING	○ FERTILIZING	○ TREE TRIMMING PRUNING
○ WEED EATING	○ BLOWING	○ POWER WASHING
○ EDGING	○ MULCHING	○ PEST CONTROL
○ HEDGE TRIMMING	○ WEEDING	○ GUTTER CLEANING
○ WATERING	○ LEAF/STRAW RAKING	○ AERATION

INSTRUCTIONS

TOOLS

INFORMATIONS

DATE: .... TIME: .... S M T W TH F S

CLIENT NAME	
PHONE NO	
EMAIL	
ADDRESS/ CITY-STATE-ZIP	

JOB FREQUENCY	WEEKLY /BI-WEEKLY	MONTHLY / BI-MONTHLY
PAYMENT PERIODS	○ WEEKLY ○ MONTHLY	○ 6-MO ○ YEARLY
FEE AMOUNT		

SERVICES

○ MOWING	○ FERTILIZING	○ TREE TRIMMING PRUNING
○ WEED EATING	○ BLOWING	○ POWER WASHING
○ EDGING	○ MULCHING	○ PEST CONTROL
○ HEDGE TRIMMING	○ WEEDING	○ GUTTER CLEANING
○ WATERING	○ LEAF/STRAW RAKING	○ AERATION

INSTRUCTIONS

TOOLS

INFORMATIONS

DATE: .... TIME: .... S M T W TH F S

CLIENT NAME	
PHONE NO	
EMAIL	
ADDRESS/ CITY-STATE-ZIP	

JOB FREQUENCY	WEEKLY /BI-WEEKLY	MONTHLY / BI-MONTHLY
PAYMENT PERIODS	⬤ WEEKLY ⬤ MONTHLY	⬤ 6-MO ⬤ YEARLY
FEE AMOUNT		

SERVICES

⬤ MOWING	⬤ FERTILIZING	⬤ TREE TRIMMING PRUNING
⬤ WEED EATING	⬤ BLOWING	⬤ POWER WASHING
⬤ EDGING	⬤ MULCHING	⬤ PEST CONTROL
⬤ HEDGE TRIMMING	⬤ WEEDING	⬤ GUTTER CLEANING
⬤ WATERING	⬤ LEAF/STRAW RAKING	⬤ AERATION

INSTRUCTIONS

TOOLS

INFORMATIONS

DATE: .... TIME: .... S M T W TH F S

CLIENT NAME	
PHONE NO	
EMAIL	
ADDRESS/ CITY-STATE-ZIP	

JOB FREQUENCY	WEEKLY /BI-WEEKLY	MONTHLY / BI-MONTHLY
PAYMENT PERIODS	○ WEEKLY ○ MONTHLY	○ 6-MO ○ YEARLY
FEE AMOUNT		

SERVICES

○ MOWING	○ FERTILIZING	○ TREE TRIMMING PRUNING
○ WEED EATING	○ BLOWING	○ POWER WASHING
○ EDGING	○ MULCHING	○ PEST CONTROL
○ HEDGE TRIMMING	○ WEEDING	○ GUTTER CLEANING
○ WATERING	○ LEAF/STRAW RAKING	○ AERATION

INSTRUCTIONS

TOOLS

INFORMATIONS

DATE: .... TIME: .... S M T W TH F S

CLIENT NAME	
PHONE NO	
EMAIL	
ADDRESS/ CITY-STATE-ZIP	

JOB FREQUENCY	WEEKLY /BI-WEEKLY	MONTHLY / BI-MONTHLY
PAYMENT PERIODS	◯ WEEKLY ◯ MONTHLY	◯ 6-MO ◯ YEARLY
FEE AMOUNT		

SERVICES

◯ MOWING   ◯ FERTILIZING   ◯ TREE TRIMMING PRUNING
◯ WEED EATING   ◯ BLOWING   ◯ POWER WASHING
◯ EDGING   ◯ MULCHING   ◯ PEST CONTROL
◯ HEDGE TRIMMING ◯ WEEDING   ◯ GUTTER CLEANING
◯ WATERING   ◯ LEAF/STRAW RAKING   ◯ AERATION

INSTRUCTIONS

TOOLS

INFORMATIONS

DATE: .... TIME: .... S M T W TH F S

CLIENT NAME	
PHONE NO	
EMAIL	
ADDRESS/ CITY-STATE-ZIP	

JOB FREQUENCY	WEEKLY /BI-WEEKLY	MONTHLY / BI-MONTHLY
PAYMENT PERIODS	○ WEEKLY ○ MONTHLY	○ 6-MO ○ YEARLY
FEE AMOUNT		

SERVICES

○ MOWING	○ FERTILIZING	○ TREE TRIMMING PRUNING
○ WEED EATING	○ BLOWING	○ POWER WASHING
○ EDGING	○ MULCHING	○ PEST CONTROL
○ HEDGE TRIMMING	○ WEEDING	○ GUTTER CLEANING
○ WATERING	○ LEAF/STRAW RAKING	○ AERATION

INSTRUCTIONS

TOOLS

INFORMATIONS

DATE: .... TIME: .... S M T W TH F S

CLIENT NAME	
PHONE NO	
EMAIL	
ADDRESS/ CITY-STATE-ZIP	

JOB FREQUENCY	WEEKLY /BI-WEEKLY	MONTHLY / BI-MONTHLY
PAYMENT PERIODS	○ WEEKLY ○ MONTHLY	○ 6-MO ○ YEARLY
FEE AMOUNT		

SERVICES

○ MOWING	○ FERTILIZING	○ TREE TRIMMING PRUNING
○ WEED EATING	○ BLOWING	○ POWER WASHING
○ EDGING	○ MULCHING	○ PEST CONTROL
○ HEDGE TRIMMING	○ WEEDING	○ GUTTER CLEANING
○ WATERING	○ LEAF/STRAW RAKING	○ AERATION

INSTRUCTIONS

TOOLS

INFORMATIONS

DATE: .... TIME: ....   S M T W TH F S

CLIENT NAME	
PHONE NO	
EMAIL	
ADDRESS/ CITY-STATE-ZIP	

JOB FREQUENCY	WEEKLY /BI-WEEKLY	MONTHLY / BI-MONTHLY
PAYMENT PERIODS	○ WEEKLY ○ MONTHLY	○ 6-MO ○ YEARLY
FEE AMOUNT		

SERVICES

○ MOWING	○ FERTILIZING	○ TREE TRIMMING PRUNING
○ WEED EATING	○ BLOWING	○ POWER WASHING
○ EDGING	○ MULCHING	○ PEST CONTROL
○ HEDGE TRIMMING	○ WEEDING	○ GUTTER CLEANING
○ WATERING	○ LEAF/STRAW RAKING	○ AERATION

INSTRUCTIONS

TOOLS

INFORMATIONS

DATE: .... TIME: .... S M T W TH F S

CLIENT NAME	
PHONE NO	
EMAIL	
ADDRESS/ CITY-STATE-ZIP	

JOB FREQUENCY	WEEKLY /BI-WEEKLY	MONTHLY / BI-MONTHLY
PAYMENT PERIODS	○ WEEKLY ○ MONTHLY	○ 6-MO ○ YEARLY
FEE AMOUNT		

SERVICES

○ MOWING	○ FERTILIZING	○ TREE TRIMMING PRUNING
○ WEED EATING	○ BLOWING	○ POWER WASHING
○ EDGING	○ MULCHING	○ PEST CONTROL
○ HEDGE TRIMMING	○ WEEDING	○ GUTTER CLEANING
○ WATERING	○ LEAF/STRAW RAKING	○ AERATION

INSTRUCTIONS

TOOLS

INFORMATIONS

DATE: .... TIME: .... S M T W TH F S

CLIENT NAME	
PHONE NO	
EMAIL	
ADDRESS/ CITY-STATE-ZIP	

JOB FREQUENCY	WEEKLY /BI-WEEKLY	MONTHLY / BI-MONTHLY
PAYMENT PERIODS	◯ WEEKLY ◯ MONTHLY	◯ 6-MO ◯ YEARLY
FEE AMOUNT		

SERVICES

◯ MOWING	◯ FERTILIZING	◯ TREE TRIMMING PRUNING
◯ WEED EATING	◯ BLOWING	◯ POWER WASHING
◯ EDGING	◯ MULCHING	◯ PEST CONTROL
◯ HEDGE TRIMMING	◯ WEEDING	◯ GUTTER CLEANING
◯ WATERING	◯ LEAF/STRAW RAKING	◯ AERATION

INSTRUCTIONS

TOOLS

INFORMATIONS

DATE: .... TIME: .... S M T W TH F S

CLIENT NAME	
PHONE NO	
EMAIL	
ADDRESS/ CITY-STATE-ZIP	

JOB FREQUENCY	WEEKLY /BI-WEEKLY	MONTHLY / BI-MONTHLY
PAYMENT PERIODS	◯ WEEKLY ◯ MONTHLY	◯ 6-MO ◯ YEARLY
FEE AMOUNT		

SERVICES

◯ MOWING
◯ WEED EATING
◯ EDGING
◯ HEDGE TRIMMING
◯ WATERING

◯ FERTILIZING
◯ BLOWING
◯ MULCHING
◯ WEEDING
◯ LEAF/STRAW RAKING

◯ TREE TRIMMING PRUNING
◯ POWER WASHING
◯ PEST CONTROL
◯ GUTTER CLEANING
◯ AERATION

INSTRUCTIONS

TOOLS

INFORMATIONS

DATE: .... TIME: ....   S   M   T   W   TH   F   S

CLIENT NAME	
PHONE NO	
EMAIL	
ADDRESS/ CITY-STATE-ZIP	

JOB FREQUENCY	WEEKLY /BI-WEEKLY	MONTHLY / BI-MONTHLY
PAYMENT PERIODS	◯ WEEKLY ◯ MONTHLY	◯ 6-MO ◯ YEARLY
FEE AMOUNT		

SERVICES

◯ MOWING	◯ FERTILIZING	◯ TREE TRIMMING PRUNING
◯ WEED EATING	◯ BLOWING	◯ POWER WASHING
◯ EDGING	◯ MULCHING	◯ PEST CONTROL
◯ HEDGE TRIMMING	◯ WEEDING	◯ GUTTER CLEANING
◯ WATERING	◯ LEAF/STRAW RAKING	◯ AERATION

INSTRUCTIONS

TOOLS

INFORMATIONS

DATE: .... TIME: .... S M T W TH F S

CLIENT NAME	
PHONE NO	
EMAIL	
ADDRESS/ CITY-STATE-ZIP	

JOB FREQUENCY	WEEKLY /BI-WEEKLY	MONTHLY / BI-MONTHLY
PAYMENT PERIODS	○ WEEKLY ○ MONTHLY	○ 6-MO ○ YEARLY
FEE AMOUNT		

SERVICES

○ MOWING	○ FERTILIZING	○ TREE TRIMMING PRUNING
○ WEED EATING	○ BLOWING	○ POWER WASHING
○ EDGING	○ MULCHING	○ PEST CONTROL
○ HEDGE TRIMMING	○ WEEDING	○ GUTTER CLEANING
○ WATERING	○ LEAF/STRAW RAKING	○ AERATION

INSTRUCTIONS

TOOLS

DATE: .... TIME: .... S M T W TH F S

CLIENT NAME	
PHONE NO	
EMAIL	
ADDRESS/ CITY-STATE-ZIP	

JOB FREQUENCY	WEEKLY /BI-WEEKLY	MONTHLY / BI-MONTHLY
PAYMENT PERIODS	○ WEEKLY ○ MONTHLY	○ 6-MO ○ YEARLY
FEE AMOUNT		

SERVICES

○ MOWING	○ FERTILIZING	○ TREE TRIMMING PRUNING
○ WEED EATING	○ BLOWING	○ POWER WASHING
○ EDGING	○ MULCHING	○ PEST CONTROL
○ HEDGE TRIMMING	○ WEEDING	○ GUTTER CLEANING
○ WATERING	○ LEAF/STRAW RAKING	○ AERATION

INSTRUCTIONS

TOOLS

INFORMATIONS

DATE: .... TIME: .... S M T W TH F S

CLIENT NAME	
PHONE NO	
EMAIL	
ADDRESS/ CITY-STATE-ZIP	

JOB FREQUENCY	WEEKLY /BI-WEEKLY	MONTHLY / BI-MONTHLY
PAYMENT PERIODS	◯ WEEKLY ◯ MONTHLY	◯ 6-MO ◯ YEARLY
FEE AMOUNT		

SERVICES

◯ MOWING	◯ FERTILIZING	◯ TREE TRIMMING PRUNING
◯ WEED EATING	◯ BLOWING	◯ POWER WASHING
◯ EDGING	◯ MULCHING	◯ PEST CONTROL
◯ HEDGE TRIMMING	◯ WEEDING	◯ GUTTER CLEANING
◯ WATERING	◯ LEAF/STRAW RAKING	◯ AERATION

INSTRUCTIONS

TOOLS

INFORMATIONS

DATE: .... TIME: .... S M T W TH F S

CLIENT NAME	
PHONE NO	
EMAIL	
ADDRESS/ CITY-STATE-ZIP	

JOB FREQUENCY	WEEKLY /BI-WEEKLY	MONTHLY / BI-MONTHLY
PAYMENT PERIODS	◯ WEEKLY ◯ MONTHLY	◯ 6-MO ◯ YEARLY
FEE AMOUNT		

SERVICES

◯ MOWING	◯ FERTILIZING	◯ TREE TRIMMING PRUNING
◯ WEED EATING	◯ BLOWING	◯ POWER WASHING
◯ EDGING	◯ MULCHING	◯ PEST CONTROL
◯ HEDGE TRIMMING	◯ WEEDING	◯ GUTTER CLEANING
◯ WATERING	◯ LEAF/STRAW RAKING	◯ AERATION

INSTRUCTIONS

TOOLS

INFORMATIONS

DATE: .... TIME: ....　　S　M　T　W　TH　F　S

CLIENT NAME	
PHONE NO	
EMAIL	
ADDRESS/ CITY-STATE-ZIP	

JOB FREQUENCY	WEEKLY /BI-WEEKLY	MONTHLY / BI-MONTHLY
PAYMENT PERIODS	○ WEEKLY　　○ MONTHLY	○ 6-MO　　○ YEARLY
FEE AMOUNT		

SERVICES

○ MOWING	○ FERTILIZING	○ TREE TRIMMING PRUNING
○ WEED EATING	○ BLOWING	○ POWER WASHING
○ EDGING	○ MULCHING	○ PEST CONTROL
○ HEDGE TRIMMING	○ WEEDING	○ GUTTER CLEANING
○ WATERING	○ LEAF/STRAW RAKING	○ AERATION

INSTRUCTIONS

TOOLS

DATE: .... TIME: .... S M T W TH F S

CLIENT NAME	
PHONE NO	
EMAIL	
ADDRESS/ CITY-STATE-ZIP	

JOB FREQUENCY	WEEKLY /BI-WEEKLY	MONTHLY / BI-MONTHLY
PAYMENT PERIODS	○ WEEKLY ○ MONTHLY	○ 6-MO ○ YEARLY
FEE AMOUNT		

SERVICES

○ MOWING	○ FERTILIZING	○ TREE TRIMMING PRUNING
○ WEED EATING	○ BLOWING	○ POWER WASHING
○ EDGING	○ MULCHING	○ PEST CONTROL
○ HEDGE TRIMMING	○ WEEDING	○ GUTTER CLEANING
○ WATERING	○ LEAF/STRAW RAKING	○ AERATION

INSTRUCTIONS

TOOLS

INFORMATIONS

DATE: .... TIME: .... S M T W TH F S

CLIENT NAME	
PHONE NO	
EMAIL	
ADDRESS/ CITY-STATE-ZIP	

JOB FREQUENCY	WEEKLY /BI-WEEKLY	MONTHLY / BI-MONTHLY
PAYMENT PERIODS	○ WEEKLY ○ MONTHLY	○ 6-MO ○ YEARLY
FEE AMOUNT		

SERVICES

○ MOWING

○ WEED EATING

○ EDGING

○ HEDGE TRIMMING

○ WATERING

○ FERTILIZING

○ BLOWING

○ MULCHING

○ WEEDING

○ LEAF/STRAW RAKING

○ TREE TRIMMING PRUNING

○ POWER WASHING

○ PEST CONTROL

○ GUTTER CLEANING

○ AERATION

INSTRUCTIONS

TOOLS

INFORMATIONS

DATE: .... TIME: .... S M T W TH F S

CLIENT NAME	
PHONE NO	
EMAIL	
ADDRESS/ CITY-STATE-ZIP	

JOB FREQUENCY	WEEKLY /BI-WEEKLY	MONTHLY / BI-MONTHLY
PAYMENT PERIODS	○ WEEKLY ○ MONTHLY	○ 6-MO ○ YEARLY
FEE AMOUNT		

SERVICES

○ MOWING	○ FERTILIZING	○ TREE TRIMMING PRUNING
○ WEED EATING	○ BLOWING	○ POWER WASHING
○ EDGING	○ MULCHING	○ PEST CONTROL
○ HEDGE TRIMMING	○ WEEDING	○ GUTTER CLEANING
○ WATERING	○ LEAF/STRAW RAKING	○ AERATION

INSTRUCTIONS

TOOLS

INFORMATIONS

DATE: .... TIME: .... S M T W TH F S

CLIENT NAME	
PHONE NO	
EMAIL	
ADDRESS/ CITY-STATE-ZIP	

JOB FREQUENCY	WEEKLY /BI-WEEKLY	MONTHLY / BI-MONTHLY
PAYMENT PERIODS	○ WEEKLY ○ MONTHLY	○ 6-MO ○ YEARLY
FEE AMOUNT		

SERVICES

○ MOWING	○ FERTILIZING	○ TREE TRIMMING PRUNING
○ WEED EATING	○ BLOWING	○ POWER WASHING
○ EDGING	○ MULCHING	○ PEST CONTROL
○ HEDGE TRIMMING	○ WEEDING	○ GUTTER CLEANING
○ WATERING	○ LEAF/STRAW RAKING	○ AERATION

INSTRUCTIONS

TOOLS

INFORMATIONS

DATE: .... TIME: .... S M T W TH F S

CLIENT NAME	
PHONE NO	
EMAIL	
ADDRESS/ CITY-STATE-ZIP	

JOB FREQUENCY	WEEKLY /BI-WEEKLY	MONTHLY / BI-MONTHLY
PAYMENT PERIODS	◯ WEEKLY ◯ MONTHLY	◯ 6-MO ◯ YEARLY
FEE AMOUNT		

SERVICES

◯ MOWING	◯ FERTILIZING	◯ TREE TRIMMING PRUNING
◯ WEED EATING	◯ BLOWING	◯ POWER WASHING
◯ EDGING	◯ MULCHING	◯ PEST CONTROL
◯ HEDGE TRIMMING	◯ WEEDING	◯ GUTTER CLEANING
◯ WATERING	◯ LEAF/STRAW RAKING	◯ AERATION

INSTRUCTIONS

TOOLS

INFORMATIONS

DATE: .... TIME: .... S M T W TH F S

CLIENT NAME	
PHONE NO	
EMAIL	
ADDRESS/ CITY-STATE-ZIP	

JOB FREQUENCY	WEEKLY /BI-WEEKLY	MONTHLY / BI-MONTHLY
PAYMENT PERIODS	○ WEEKLY ○ MONTHLY	○ 6-MO ○ YEARLY
FEE AMOUNT		

SERVICES

○ MOWING	○ FERTILIZING	○ TREE TRIMMING PRUNING
○ WEED EATING	○ BLOWING	○ POWER WASHING
○ EDGING	○ MULCHING	○ PEST CONTROL
○ HEDGE TRIMMING	○ WEEDING	○ GUTTER CLEANING
○ WATERING	○ LEAF/STRAW RAKING	○ AERATION

INSTRUCTIONS

TOOLS

INFORMATIONS

DATE: .... TIME: .... S M T W TH F S

CLIENT NAME	
PHONE NO	
EMAIL	
ADDRESS/ CITY-STATE-ZIP	

JOB FREQUENCY	WEEKLY /BI-WEEKLY	MONTHLY / BI-MONTHLY
PAYMENT PERIODS	○ WEEKLY ○ MONTHLY	○ 6-MO ○ YEARLY
FEE AMOUNT		

SERVICES

○ MOWING	○ FERTILIZING	○ TREE TRIMMING PRUNING
○ WEED EATING	○ BLOWING	○ POWER WASHING
○ EDGING	○ MULCHING	○ PEST CONTROL
○ HEDGE TRIMMING	○ WEEDING	○ GUTTER CLEANING
○ WATERING	○ LEAF/STRAW RAKING	○ AERATION

INSTRUCTIONS

TOOLS

INFORMATIONS

DATE: .... TIME: .... S M T W TH F S

CLIENT NAME	
PHONE NO	
EMAIL	
ADDRESS/ CITY-STATE-ZIP	

JOB FREQUENCY	WEEKLY /BI-WEEKLY	MONTHLY / BI-MONTHLY
PAYMENT PERIODS	◯ WEEKLY ◯ MONTHLY	◯ 6-MO ◯ YEARLY
FEE AMOUNT		

SERVICES

◯ MOWING	◯ FERTILIZING	◯ TREE TRIMMING PRUNING
◯ WEED EATING	◯ BLOWING	◯ POWER WASHING
◯ EDGING	◯ MULCHING	◯ PEST CONTROL
◯ HEDGE TRIMMING	◯ WEEDING	◯ GUTTER CLEANING
◯ WATERING	◯ LEAF/STRAW RAKING	◯ AERATION

INSTRUCTIONS

TOOLS

INFORMATIONS

DATE: .... TIME: .... S M T W TH F S

CLIENT NAME	
PHONE NO	
EMAIL	
ADDRESS/ CITY-STATE-ZIP	

JOB FREQUENCY	WEEKLY /BI-WEEKLY	MONTHLY / BI-MONTHLY
PAYMENT PERIODS	○ WEEKLY ○ MONTHLY	○ 6-MO ○ YEARLY
FEE AMOUNT		

SERVICES

○ MOWING	○ FERTILIZING	○ TREE TRIMMING PRUNING
○ WEED EATING	○ BLOWING	○ POWER WASHING
○ EDGING	○ MULCHING	○ PEST CONTROL
○ HEDGE TRIMMING	○ WEEDING	○ GUTTER CLEANING
○ WATERING	○ LEAF/STRAW RAKING	○ AERATION

INSTRUCTIONS

TOOLS

INFORMATIONS

DATE: .... TIME: .... S M T W TH F S

CLIENT NAME	
PHONE NO	
EMAIL	
ADDRESS/ CITY-STATE-ZIP	

JOB FREQUENCY	WEEKLY /BI-WEEKLY	MONTHLY / BI-MONTHLY
PAYMENT PERIODS	○ WEEKLY ○ MONTHLY	○ 6-MO ○ YEARLY
FEE AMOUNT		

SERVICES

○ MOWING	○ FERTILIZING	○ TREE TRIMMING PRUNING
○ WEED EATING	○ BLOWING	○ POWER WASHING
○ EDGING	○ MULCHING	○ PEST CONTROL
○ HEDGE TRIMMING	○ WEEDING	○ GUTTER CLEANING
○ WATERING	○ LEAF/STRAW RAKING	○ AERATION

INSTRUCTIONS

TOOLS

INFORMATIONS

DATE: .... TIME: .... S M T W TH F S

CLIENT NAME	
PHONE NO	
EMAIL	
ADDRESS/ CITY-STATE-ZIP	

JOB FREQUENCY	WEEKLY /BI-WEEKLY	MONTHLY / BI-MONTHLY
PAYMENT PERIODS	○ WEEKLY ○ MONTHLY	○ 6-MO ○ YEARLY
FEE AMOUNT		

SERVICES

○ MOWING	○ FERTILIZING	○ TREE TRIMMING PRUNING
○ WEED EATING	○ BLOWING	○ POWER WASHING
○ EDGING	○ MULCHING	○ PEST CONTROL
○ HEDGE TRIMMING	○ WEEDING	○ GUTTER CLEANING
○ WATERING	○ LEAF/STRAW RAKING	○ AERATION

INSTRUCTIONS

TOOLS

INFORMATIONS

DATE: .... TIME: .... S M T W TH F S

CLIENT NAME	
PHONE NO	
EMAIL	
ADDRESS/ CITY-STATE-ZIP	

JOB FREQUENCY	WEEKLY /BI-WEEKLY	MONTHLY / BI-MONTHLY
PAYMENT PERIODS	○ WEEKLY ○ MONTHLY	○ 6-MO ○ YEARLY
FEE AMOUNT		

SERVICES

○ MOWING	○ FERTILIZING	○ TREE TRIMMING PRUNING
○ WEED EATING	○ BLOWING	○ POWER WASHING
○ EDGING	○ MULCHING	○ PEST CONTROL
○ HEDGE TRIMMING	○ WEEDING	○ GUTTER CLEANING
○ WATERING	○ LEAF/STRAW RAKING	○ AERATION

INSTRUCTIONS

TOOLS

INFORMATIONS

DATE: .... TIME: .... S M T W TH F S

CLIENT NAME	
PHONE NO	
EMAIL	
ADDRESS/ CITY-STATE-ZIP	

JOB FREQUENCY	WEEKLY /BI-WEEKLY	MONTHLY / BI-MONTHLY
PAYMENT PERIODS	◯ WEEKLY ◯ MONTHLY	◯ 6-MO ◯ YEARLY
FEE AMOUNT		

SERVICES

◯ MOWING	◯ FERTILIZING	◯ TREE TRIMMING PRUNING
◯ WEED EATING	◯ BLOWING	◯ POWER WASHING
◯ EDGING	◯ MULCHING	◯ PEST CONTROL
◯ HEDGE TRIMMING	◯ WEEDING	◯ GUTTER CLEANING
◯ WATERING	◯ LEAF/STRAW RAKING	◯ AERATION

INSTRUCTIONS

TOOLS

INFORMATIONS

DATE: .... TIME: .... S M T W TH F S

CLIENT NAME	
PHONE NO	
EMAIL	
ADDRESS/ CITY-STATE-ZIP	

JOB FREQUENCY	WEEKLY /BI-WEEKLY	MONTHLY / BI-MONTHLY
PAYMENT PERIODS	○ WEEKLY ○ MONTHLY	○ 6-MO ○ YEARLY
FEE AMOUNT		

SERVICES

○ MOWING	○ FERTILIZING	○ TREE TRIMMING PRUNING
○ WEED EATING	○ BLOWING	○ POWER WASHING
○ EDGING	○ MULCHING	○ PEST CONTROL
○ HEDGE TRIMMING	○ WEEDING	○ GUTTER CLEANING
○ WATERING	○ LEAF/STRAW RAKING	○ AERATION

INSTRUCTIONS

TOOLS

INFORMATIONS

DATE: .... TIME: .... S M T W TH F S

CLIENT NAME	
PHONE NO	
EMAIL	
ADDRESS/ CITY-STATE-ZIP	

JOB FREQUENCY	WEEKLY /BI-WEEKLY	MONTHLY / BI-MONTHLY
PAYMENT PERIODS	○ WEEKLY ○ MONTHLY	○ 6-MO ○ YEARLY
FEE AMOUNT		

SERVICES

○ MOWING	○ FERTILIZING	○ TREE TRIMMING PRUNING
○ WEED EATING	○ BLOWING	○ POWER WASHING
○ EDGING	○ MULCHING	○ PEST CONTROL
○ HEDGE TRIMMING	○ WEEDING	○ GUTTER CLEANING
○ WATERING	○ LEAF/STRAW RAKING	○ AERATION

INSTRUCTIONS

TOOLS

INFORMATIONS

DATE: .... TIME: .... S M T W TH F S

CLIENT NAME	
PHONE NO	
EMAIL	
ADDRESS/ CITY-STATE-ZIP	

JOB FREQUENCY	WEEKLY /BI-WEEKLY	MONTHLY / BI-MONTHLY
PAYMENT PERIODS	○ WEEKLY ○ MONTHLY	○ 6-MO ○ YEARLY
FEE AMOUNT		

SERVICES

○ MOWING	○ FERTILIZING	○ TREE TRIMMING PRUNING
○ WEED EATING	○ BLOWING	○ POWER WASHING
○ EDGING	○ MULCHING	○ PEST CONTROL
○ HEDGE TRIMMING	○ WEEDING	○ GUTTER CLEANING
○ WATERING	○ LEAF/STRAW RAKING	○ AERATION

INSTRUCTIONS

TOOLS

INFORMATIONS

DATE: .... TIME: .... S M T W TH F S

CLIENT NAME	
PHONE NO	
EMAIL	
ADDRESS/ CITY-STATE-ZIP	

JOB FREQUENCY	WEEKLY /BI-WEEKLY	MONTHLY / BI-MONTHLY
PAYMENT PERIODS	○ WEEKLY ○ MONTHLY	○ 6-MO ○ YEARLY
FEE AMOUNT		

SERVICES

○ MOWING	○ FERTILIZING	○ TREE TRIMMING PRUNING
○ WEED EATING	○ BLOWING	○ POWER WASHING
○ EDGING	○ MULCHING	○ PEST CONTROL
○ HEDGE TRIMMING	○ WEEDING	○ GUTTER CLEANING
○ WATERING	○ LEAF/STRAW RAKING	○ AERATION

INSTRUCTIONS

TOOLS

INFORMATIONS

DATE: .... TIME: .... S M T W TH F S

CLIENT NAME	
PHONE NO	
EMAIL	
ADDRESS/ CITY-STATE-ZIP	

JOB FREQUENCY	WEEKLY /BI-WEEKLY	MONTHLY / BI-MONTHLY
PAYMENT PERIODS	◯ WEEKLY ◯ MONTHLY	◯ 6-MO ◯ YEARLY
FEE AMOUNT		

SERVICES

◯ MOWING	◯ FERTILIZING	◯ TREE TRIMMING PRUNING
◯ WEED EATING	◯ BLOWING	◯ POWER WASHING
◯ EDGING	◯ MULCHING	◯ PEST CONTROL
◯ HEDGE TRIMMING	◯ WEEDING	◯ GUTTER CLEANING
◯ WATERING	◯ LEAF/STRAW RAKING	◯ AERATION

INSTRUCTIONS

TOOLS